A00364453

D1613132

BUILDING A WORLD-CLASS NHS

Ian Smith

First published 2007 by
PALGRAVE MACMILLAN
Houndmills, Basingstoke, Hampshire RG21 6XS and
175 Fifth Avenue, New York, N.Y. 10010
Companies and representatives throughout the world

PALGRAVE MACMILLAN is the global academic imprint of the Palgrave Macmillan division of St. Martin's Press, LLC and of Palgrave Macmillan Ltd. Macmillan® is a registered trademark in the United States, United Kingdom and other countries. Palgrave is a registered trademark in the European Union and other countries.

ISBN-13: 978-0-230-55380-4
ISBN-10: 0-230-55380-X

This book is printed on paper suitable for recycling and made from fully managed and sustained forest sources. Logging, pulping and manufacturing processes are expected to conform to the environmental regulations of the country of origin.

A catalogue record for this book is available from the British Library.

A catalog record for this book is available from the Library of Congress.

10   9   8   7   6   5   4   3   2   1
16   15   14   13   12   11   10   09   08   07

Printed and bound in China

Contents

List of Tables and Figures

Tables

Figures

Acknowledgements

Carol Friend, Trevor Jones and Laura Wilson helped me considerably in writing this book. Their practical and moral support are greatly appreciated. Keith Povey and Julene Knox, the former as general editor and the latter as permissions editor, have been very patient with the novice author that I am. Palgrave Macmillan, especially Alex Dawe, has been very generous in support of this book. My brother, Professor Stephen Smith, Principal of Imperial College Medical School, and a NHS employee for over 30 years, has been very helpful, especially in providing the clinical perspective on a number of matters. I should stress that he does not agree with all of my conclusions in this book, but his overall perspective has been very helpful. I have also been hugely impressed with his unerring concern for his patients, a dedication which he has consistently demonstrated since he entered medicine in 1969. Stephen is, in this important respect, a very typical clinician. I would also like to thank Professor Nick Bosanquet, who has been both influential in my thinking and highly supportive of my views. Through Nick's efforts, also, the think-tank Reform has encouraged me in my efforts, and has published a pamphlet version of this book. I am also very grateful to Professor Michael Porter of the Harvard Business School. I have known Mike for over twenty years and have had the privilege of working with him in the past. His new book on healthcare (*Redefining Healthcare*) is excellent and forms an important central theme to my book.

IAN SMITH

The author and publishers are grateful to the following for permission to reproduce copyright material. If any have been inadvertently omitted the publishers will make the necessary arrangement at the earliest opportunity.

Introduction

'Big increases in NHS Funding'. Chart on health spending from Department of Health, Treasury Website http://www.ifs.org.uk/budgets/budget2007/bma_presentation.ppt#368,22,Healthspending. Reproduced under the terms of the Click-Use Licence (Licence no. C2007001306).

'Framework for the Reforms' by Bill McCarthy. Figure from 'Health Reform in England: Update and Next Steps'. Presentation available on DOH website. Reproduced under the terms of the Click-Use Licence (Licence no. C2007001306).

Excerpts and charts from *The Quest for Quality in the NHS: A Chartbook on Quality of Care in the UK*, by Sheila Leatherman and Kim Sutherland, 2005, The Nuffield Trust. Reproduced with permission from Radcliffe Publishing Ltd.

'Expansion of NHS capacity' (1.3 NHS and IS Treatment Centre Scheme Locations). Figure reprinted by permissions of Rothschild–London.

Excerpts reprinted by permission of Harvard Business School Press. From Porter, Michael E. and Teisberg, Elizabeth Olmsted (2006), *Redefining Healthcare: Creating Value-Based Competition on Results*, Boston, Massachusetts, 2006. Copyright © 2006 by the Harvard Business School Publishing Corporation.

'NHS Future Spending vs. NHS Current Spending' and 'Breakdown of Additional Spend'. Charts from Western Provident Association http://www.wpa.org.uk/. Reproduced with permission.

Chapter 1

'The NHS is making Progress: Maximum Inpatient Waiting Times', chart from Chief Executives Report to the NHS, 2004 [3] http://www.dh.gov.uk/en/Publicationsandstatistics/Publications/PublicationsPolicy AndGuidance/DH_4081823. Reproduced under the terms of the Click-Use Licence (Licence no. C2007001306).

'News investigation: This year's NHS bill is pounds 87bn . . . so just where did the cash go?: All new spending on the NHS has been blocked, as we reveal on the front page. How could a multi-billion pound increase in funding fail to prevent closed wards and cancelled operations?', Jo Revill reports, Jo Revill, 11 December 2005 Copyright Guardian News & Media Ltd 2005.

Excerpts and chart from King's Fund Briefing, *Where's the Money Going?*, Page 2, February 2006. Reproduced with permission.

'Hospital Hailed as Future of the NHS is Forced to Close', *The Times*, 30 August 2006. © 2006 NI Syndication, London.

'Debt-ridden Trusts Halt IVF Treatment', Sarah Hall, Health correspondent, 13 September 2006 Copyright Guardian News & Media Ltd 2006.

'NHS Trusts with Deficits of over £5 million', chart from Audited accounts of NHS Trusts [6] 'Financial Management in the NHS', joint report by the National Audit Office and the Audit Commission, June 2005. Reproduced under the terms of the Click-Use Licence (Licence no. C2007001306).

'Thrombolysis rates post-acute myocardial infarction, England 2002–04', chart from Royal College of Physicians, *How the NHS Manages Heart Attacks: Third Public Report of the Myocardial Infarction National Audit Project (MINAP)*, London: Royal College of Physicians, 2005. Reproduced with permission.

'Wait in Accident and Emergency, international comparison', 'Breast Cancer Mortality Rates: International Comparison 1990 and 1999', 'Breast Cancer Survival (1992–1997) and Screening Rates (2000), International Comparison', 'Hospitals Rated Excellent at Finding and Addressing Medical Error, International Comparison, 2000', 'Physicians' Ratings of Hospital Effectiveness in Finding and Addressing Medical Error, UK 2000', data from Commonwealth Fund International Survey 2004. Reproduced by kind permission of The Commonwealth Fund, www.commonwealthfund.org.

'Mortality Rates from Circulatory Disease UK 1971–2002', data from Office of National Statistics 2004, reproduced under the terms of the Click-Use Licence (Licence no. C2007001306).

'Mortality Rates from Coronary Heart Disease (35–74 years), International Comparison 1999–2000', data from WHO Mortality Database. Reproduced by kind permission of WHO Press, Publishing Policy Review Group, World Health Organization.

'Mortality Rates from Coronary Heart Disease, males 35–74 years, UK countries 1997–2000' and 'Mortality Rates from Coronary Heart Disease, Females 35–74 years, UK countries 1997–2002', data from HeartStats ONS data. Reproduced under the terms of the Click-Use Licence (Licence no. C2007001306).

'Contributing Factors in the Decline in Coronary Heart Disease Mortality, England and Wales 1981–2000 (%)', chart from Unal, B., Critchley, J.A. and Capewell, S. (2004) 'Explaining the Decline in Coronary Heart Disease Mortality in England and Wales between 1981 and 2000', *Circulation*, 109(9): 1101–7. Reproduced by permission of Lippincott Williams & Wilkins/Wolters Kluwer Health.

'Proportion of Death Prevented or Postponed as a Result of Population Risk Factor Changes', chart from Unal, B., Critchley, J.A. and Capewell, S. (2004) 'Explaining the Decline in Coronary Heart Disease Mortality in England and Wales between 1981 and 2000', *Circulation*, 109(9): 1101–7. Reproduced by permission of Lippincott Williams & Wilkins/Wolters Kluwer Health.

'Breast Screening Coverage on Women aged 50–64, UK Countries 1992–2002', data from Office of National Statistics. Reproduced under the terms of the Click-Use Licence (Licence no. C2007001306).

'MRSA Bacteraemia as a Proportion of all *Staphylococcuus aureus* bacteraemias, International Comparison, 1999–2002', chart from Tiemersma, E.W., Bronzwaer, S.L., Lyytikainen, O. *et al.* (2004), 'European Antimicrobial Resistance Surveillance System Participants Methicillin-resistant Staphylococcus aureus in Europe, 1999–2002', *Emerging Infectious Diseases*, 10(9): 1627–34, published by Centers for Disease Control and Prevention.

Excerpts from The Bristol Report, http://www.bristol-inquiry.org.uk/index.htm. Reproduced under the terms of the Click-Use Licence (Licence no. C2007001306).

'Rights of Arrogant Surgeons Risk Another Bristol Babies Scandals', *The Sunday Times*, 13.9.2006. © 2006 NI Syndication, London.

'After Years of Poor Management and Underinvestment', 'UK Citizens Feel that there are Better Systems Elsewhere in Europe', 'UK Citizens Judge the NHS Poorly . . .', and 'UK Citizens also Judge the NHS Poorly on Doctor Choice', charts from *Impatient for Change: European Attitudes to Healthcare reform*, Stockholm Network and Populus 2004. Reproduced with permission.

Chapter 2

Excerpts from Alan Milburn, a former Minister of Health, Speech to the New Health Network, 14 January 2002. Reproduced under the terms of the Click-Use Licence (Licence no. C2007001306).

Excerpts from 'End of NHS reforms or my members may vote Tory, warns union chief', *Daily Telegraph*, 9/9/06, p. 4 copyright © Toby Helm/ The Daily Telegraph, reproduced with permission.

'Which words do you think apply to public services in Britain these days?', Ipsos MORI (2005) survey of 2000 aged 16+, from Ipsos MORI Social Research Institute End of Year Report, 2005. Reproduced with permission.

Excerpts from Ken Jarrold, Sally Irvine Lecture, 'The NHS – Past, Present and Future', Tuesday 15 November 2005, IHM Annual Conference and Exhibition. Reproduced by kind permission of Ken Jarrold.

Excerpts from Audit Commission, Page 2, 'Early Lessons from Payment by Result', 11 October 2005. Reproduced under the terms of the Click-Use Licence (Licence no. C2007001306).

Hewitt demands more rigour in NHS investment: Trusts accused of taking unaffordable decisions Business plans to be required for spending, John Carvel, Social affairs editor, 12 September 2006, Copyright Guardian News & Media Ltd 2006.

Excerpts from OECD Economic Surveys: United Kingdom, 'Activity-Based Funding, Incentives and Waiting Times in Health Care', Volume 2004 Issue 3, © OECD 2004. Reproduced with permission.

Excerpts from Patricia Hewitt, *Annual Health and Social Care Lecture*, LSE, 13 December 2005. Reproduced under the terms of the Click-Use Licence (Licence no. C2007001306).

'Ministers Pin Hopes on Ambitious 18-week Maximum Wait for Surgery', Nicholas Timmins, *Financial Times*, 4 January 2006; and 'NHS Fails Tests on Improved Efficiency', FT.com 18 October 2004. Reproduced by permission of the Financial Times.

Excerpts from OECD Economic Surveys: United Kingdom – Volume 2005 Supplement 2, © OECD 2005. Reproduced with permission.

Excerpts from 'NHS Productivity Report "Misses Crucial Changes"', 22 October 2004, page 1, *Public Finance*, The Statistics Commission. Reproduced with permission.

Excerpts from Professor Julian Le Grand, *Guardian Unlimited*, page 2, 'Market Forces are the Future of the Health Service', 26 September 2005. Reproduced by kind permission of Julian Le Grand.

Excerpts from *Public Service Productivy: Health*, Office of National Statistics 2006. Reproduced under the terms of the Click-Use Licence (Licence no. C2007001306).

Excerpt from National Audit Office and the Audit Commission, page 7, 'Financial Management in the NHS', 24 June 2005. Reproduced under the terms of the Click-Use Licence (Licence no. C2007001306).

Excerpts from Audit Commission, page 25, 'Managing the Financial Implications of NICE Guidance', September 2005. Reproduced under the terms of the Click-Use Licence (Licence no. C2007001306).

Excerpts from 'Financial Turnaround in the NHS', page 4, Department of Health, 25 January 2005. Reproduced under the terms of the Click-Use Licence (Licence no. C2007001306).

Chart showing 'Relationship between Health Benefits and Health Spending' from King's Fund, *Spending on Health Care: How Much is Enough?*, John Appleby and Anthony Harrison, February 2006. Reproduced with permission.

'NHS Career Path is a Short One', *The Times*, 12.9.2006. © 2006 NI Syndication, London.

Comment & Analysis: Even Nye Bevan's NHS saw a role for the private sector: To accuse the government of privatising the health service is absurd, Patricia Hewitt, 2 July 2005. Copyright Guardian News & Media Ltd 2005.

Excerpts from 'The Reluctant Managers Part 1: Report on Reforming Whitehall', December 2005, published by KPMG. Reproduced with permission.

Chapter 3

'The Care Delivery Value Chain', 'The Virtuous Circle in a Medical Condition', and 'Boston Spine Group', charts reprinted by permission of Harvard Business School Press. From Porter, Michael E. and Teisberg, Elizabeth Olmsted (2006), *Redefining Healthcare: Creating Value-Based Competition on Results*, Boston, Massachusetts, 2006. Copyright © 2006 by the Harvard Business School Publishing Corporation.

Chapter 4

Excerpts from Julian Le Grand, 'Choice and Competition in Public Services, Public Lecture', London School of Economics, 21 February 2006. Reproduced by kind permission of Julian Le Grand.

'Who Wants Choice: Gender'; 'Should Patients Have Choice?'; 'Who Wants Choice: Social Class'; 'Who Wants Choice: Income'; 'Who Wants Choice: Educational Qualification', charts reproduced with permission from John Appleby and Arturo Alvarez, *Public Responses to NHS Reform, British Social Attitudes Survey 22nd Report*, Copyright © John Appleby and Arturo Alvarez 2005, by permission of Sage Publications Ltd.

'Wanted: A Battle-hardened manager for NHS', Nicholas Timmins, *Financial Times*, 8 March 2006. Reproduced by permission of the Financial Times.

Excerpts from Professor Paul Corrigan, 'Improving the Quality and Capacity of Primary Care', Social Market Foundations, November 2005. Reproduced with permission.

Excerpts from King's Fund, Page 1, NHS Waiting Times, 1 April 2005 (available from http://www.kings-fund.org.uk/publications/briefings/nhs_waiting.html). Reproduced with permission.

'The Government is Developing a New Policy to Offer People Using the NHS More Choice'. Table from *Patient Choice*, 'Final Topline Results', 1 February 2005 (data later published in Research study conducted for Department of Health, Report 7 October 2005. Ben Page and Andy Byrom MORI Social Research Institute). Reproduced by permission of Ipsos MORI, www.ipsos-mori.com.

Excerpts from Department of Health, page 1, Independent Sector Treatment Centres, 16 February 2006, Ken Anderson, Commercial Director, Department of Health. Reproduced under the terms of the Click-Use Licence (Licence no. C2007001306).

Excerpts from Timmins, N. (ed.), *Designing the New NHS: Ideas to Make a Supplier Market in Health Care Work*, London: King's Fund, 2006. Reproduced with permission.

Chapter 5

Excerpts from *Strategic Science Provision in English Universities*, Science and Technology Select Committee, 2005, pp. 62, 65, 67, 79, 85. Parliamentary material is reproduced with the permission of the Controller of HMSO on behalf of Parliament (Parliamentary Licence No. P2007000193).

'The Diamond', adapted with permission of The Free Press, a Division of Simon & Schuster Adult Publishing Group, from *The Competitive Advantage of Nations* by Michael E. Porter, copyright © 1990, 1998 by Michael E. Porter, all rights reserved.

Excerpts from *A Competitive Analysis of the Healthcare Industry in the UK*, June 2001, Comap 1/2, ABHI/Eurostrategy Consultants, pp. 3, 4, 5, 7, 8, 9. Reproduced with permission.

'Summary of the Business Environment of the New Jersey Life Science Super-cluster'. Reproduced with permission from *Survey Results* http://www.isc.hbs,edu/pdf/NJ_lifescience.pdf

Introduction

Key points

1   The Labour government is committed to reforming a badly under-
    performing National Health Service (NHS). Much of what the
    government is doing is right:
    1.1   Putting money into the system; and
    1.2   Introducing sensible policy.
2   The money will be wasted and sensible policy will bring confusion
    if the biggest remaining problem of the NHS is not solved; that
    problem is the dysfunctional organization and poor management
    at all levels (up to the politicians themselves).
    2.1   Senior NHS management (and more broadly, the Civil
          Service) are, at best, lukewarm about reform, and not
          competent to manage change;
    2.2   Clinicians at all levels are prevented from using their
          expertise to improve patient care and, worse, feel delib-
          erately excluded from management despite being respon-
          sible for more than 75 per cent of healthcare expenditure;
          and
    2.3   As a consequence, there is no coherent change programme
          for one of the biggest change processes in modern history.
3   Core to a coherent change programme is a **vision** of where the
    process is heading. This is lacking.
    3.1   What it should define is a relentless focus on **patient value**
          (clinical outcomes for defined medical conditions over a full
          cycle of care per unit cost); and
    3.2   Unrestrained competition between providers to deliver ever-
          improving **patient value**.
4   Although the government's policy is largely right, it lacks the rally-
    ing cry that this **vision** provides, and worse, has not involved the
    very people – the clinicians – who deliver the care. Other policy
    gaps – although the government is working on these – are reform
    in the primary healthcare sector and in commissioning.
5   Once the **vision** is defined, and clinicians in particular are signed
    up to it, then a coherent change programme needs to be put in
    place if the reform programme is not to fail, and that programme

needs to address urgently the dysfunctional organization and poor
quality of management:

5.1   The system needs to be decentralized, de-bureaucratized
      and depoliticized;

5.2   Demand-side mechanisms need to be extended and
      strengthened – transparency of outcome data, patient
      choice, reform in primary care, and effective commissioning;

5.3   Unrestrained competition should be introduced in order to
      serve patients' interests. Despite 'privatization' scare-
      mongering, most of this competition should, and will, come
      from the Foundation Trusts rather than the tiny private
      sector; and

5.4   Senior NHS/Civil Service management positions need to be
      filled by people who have experience both of managing large
      change projects and focusing on customer value in the
      private sector.

6 The healthcare economy needs to be structured so that the focus
   on **patient value** becomes self-sustaining. A major task over the
   coming years is to build this decentralized, patient/clinician-
   responsive market:

6.1   The ultimate objective of the change programme is to create
      a healthcare economy structured so that the various actors
      are motivated on a 'day-to-day' level to maximize **patient
      value**; and

6.2   The commissioning role is crucial – the commissioners will
      be the 'market-makers'.

7 At this point we can begin to rebuild the United Kingdom's (UK's)
   lost international competitiveness in healthcare – with significant
   benefits for the UK economy.

At the time of writing it is approaching sixty years since the NHS was
created, and during this period, a service that was the envy of the world
has declined dangerously. The UK produces some of the worst health
outcomes of any developed country, and the system is insular, inward-
looking and extravagantly wasteful. Clinicians – doctors and nurses –
remain hugely committed to their patients. They put in long and stressful
hours. But they are being let down by a system that is dysfunctional. This
government has bravely decided to take on this dysfunction – it was, led

by the former prime minister,Tony Blair, committed to reform. It should be congratulated hugely for taking on such a thankless task. Many of its reforms are absolutely right, and its commitment and good intentions are beyond reproach. However, the reform process is in mortal danger of failing. The objective of this book is to offer the government recommendations as to how the reform process can be saved from failure. The stakes are high – if reform fails now, then the healthcare of two or three generations to come will be compromised. I believe passionately in the National Health Service. It will only survive, and be true to its founding principles, if the reform programme is driven forward, and if the recommendations in this book are implemented.

These are the principles I believe should underpin the NHS:

- Free at the point of need.
- Paid for from taxes to a single tariff.
- Delivering high quality, efficient and transparent clinical and 'public health' outcomes. The core objective of the healthcare system is constantly to improve **patient value** – defined as the clinical outcome for defined medical conditions over a full cycle of care, and at the best cost.
- Delivery of healthcare should be subject to the choice of the citizen who, acting on fully transparent and available information, can put poor (dangerous) performers 'out of business'.
- Unrestrained competition at the level of **patient value**, so that good performers can quickly and easily replace poor performers. The right to provide care should be based on performance in delivering **patient value**, and not on being a public sector organization.

These, in essence, are Aneurin ('Nye') Bevan's founding principles for the NHS.

Over the decades, we have moved away from these principles. The rights of the patient and the citizen have been usurped by the rights of the providers – the public-sector Civil Servants who operate a customer-unfriendly monopoly – a monopoly that protects their 'right' to job security and a big pension; a monopoly that protects them from being held accountable; and, in particular, a monopoly that protects them from the disciplining effects of competition (competition that roots out poor performers).

The Civil Service is, inevitably, lukewarm about reform, because reform is deeply threatening to their privileges. The unions claim that the reforms the government is trying to introduce are 'privatization', and that the government is betraying Bevan's founding principles. On the contrary, it is *they* who have betrayed the founding principles, and it is this government's reforms that are getting us back to the basics – to a National Health Service that serves the British people, and not the sectional interests of monopoly providers. Doctors and nurses labour every day in a system that is poorly managed,and has some of the most dysfunctional organizational dynamics of any organization in the world. This is not what Bevan intended. We are at a crossroads – we have to dismantle the NHS monopoly; we have to create a system that operates in the interests of patients and taxpayers; and we have to create an organizational dynamic that supports the good managers in doing their job, and is intolerant of poor management at all levels.

We now have an opportunity to rebuild a world-class NHS. If we fail now, we run the risk of failing for ever. Far from it being the reforms that will create 'privatization' – the failure of reform will, in fact, create privatization as people become increasingly frustrated by, and even scared of, a system that is underperforming, and then choose to spend their own money to purchase this vital service privately.

The path to failure

Since 1948, three things have degraded the NHS:

1. It has been chronically underfunded. In 1993, the UK spent 6.9 per cent of gross domestic product (GDP) on healthcare, compared to 9.4 per cent in France, 8.6 per cent in Sweden, 9.4 per cent in Switzerland and 9.9 per cent in Germany.[1]
2. It has lacked 'policy' in the sense of any guiding or aligning principles to make things work effectively, and to guide resources (money and clinical expertise) to where they are most needed. There was no explicit way, for example, of making trade-offs in the allocation of resources or controlling costs. In

£

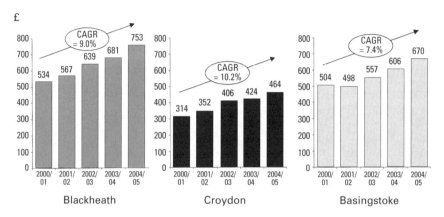

Blackheath   Croydon   Basingstoke

Notes: Weightings based on percentage of BMI admissions made from those trusts in 2005. Spend per head is from following NHS trusts: at Blackheath – Guy's and St Thomas's, King's College Hospital, Bromley Hospitals, Queen Mary's Sidcup, Greenwich Healthcare/Queen Elizabeth, Lewisham Hospital, Dartford & Gravesham; at Croydon – Mayday, St George's, Surrey & Sussex; at Basingstoke – Frimley Park & North Hampshire.
Source: Local Trust Annual Accounts (available from the Department of Health).

Figure I.1 Weighted NHS spend per head, 2000–2005

the absence of explicit policy, implicit, arbitrary and inconsistent mechanisms evolved and became embedded in the NHS. In the absence of explicit policy and decision-making, there is hidden rationing of treatments and, ironically in a service that claims to be 'for the people', ever-increasing health inequalities. The hard fact of the matter is that the white middle classes discovered how to find their way through the system, but the underprivileged got what they were given. NHS spending per capita, for example, is more than 50 per cent higher in the wealthy, middle-class towns of Basingstoke and Blackheath, compared to working-class Croydon (as Figure I.1 shows). Reform of the NHS and the eradication of health inequalities go hand in hand.

3. The NHS has become a centralized, Civil Service bureaucracy with chronically poor management and dysfunctional organizational dynamics.

Since 1997, the government has made excellent progress: NHS funding has doubled and will soon be three times what it was at the end of the

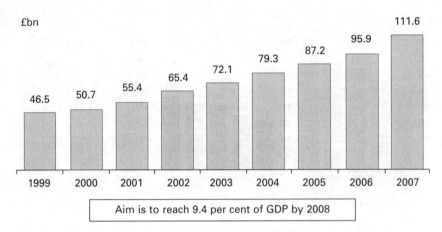

Source: Department of Health government expenditure plans; Treasury website, www.ifs.org.uk/
budgets/budget2007/bma_presentation.ppt#368,22,Health spending.

Figure I.2   Large increases in NHS funding

1990s, as Figure I.2 shows. Policy largely hangs together now and is
increasingly well articulated by people such as Paul Corrigan (former
Health Adviser to Number 10) and Bill McCarthy (former Head of Policy
at the Department of Health). Bill McCarthy's framework is shown in
Figure I.3.

This framework is good, but it needs improving. Although the individual parts of the policy agenda make sense, it lacks a unifying theme. In
this book I shall outline why **patient value** and 'unrestrained competition'
to increase **patient value** should be those unifying themes. **But,** and it is
the key 'but' explored in this book as well as the key flaw in the reform
process, the problem of a centralized bureaucracy with its chronically
poor management has not been addressed.

If the NHS is not reformed, it will terminally undermine the government's funding and policy achievements.

Pouring money into an unreformed, poorly managed system has
inevitably created waste – and will continue to do so. Although there has
been a lot of talk recently about deficits (a serious failure of management,
given that funding has nearly trebled since 1997), the really shocking fact
is that too little of this extra funding has in fact got through to improve
patient value. It has either been spent on bigger salaries for the providers,
the employment of more administrators or, more generally, wasted.

Pouring policy into this unreformed, poorly managed system has

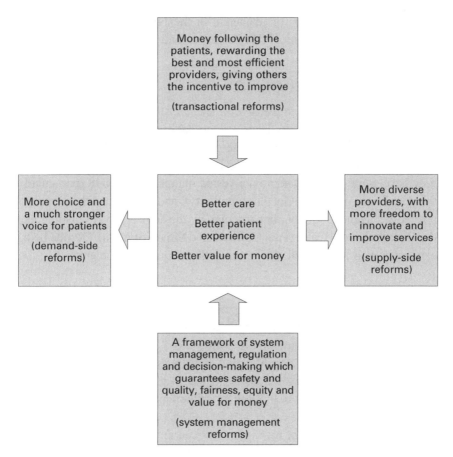

Source: Department of Health 'Framework for the Reforms' by Bill McCarthy, figure from 'Health Reform in England: update and next steps'.

Figure I.3 Framework for the reforms

created, at best, confusion and, at worst, unproductive game-playing by the smarter players. For example, there is the Accident & Emergency game of inappropriately admitting patients into hospital in order to hit the four-hour target – this game achieves targets but wastes resources and does not increase **patient value**.

The vital missing ingredient in the reform process is management and organizational change. Reform of the NHS – which employs 1.4 million people – is a massive change programme. Yet there is no explicit programme of change, and an absence of competent management to bring about the change.

There are three groups of managers in the NHS: politicians and their advisers; civil servants/senior NHS managers; and front-line NHS managers.

Politicians and their advisers

These people are hugely impressive in terms of their intelligence and their commitment to reform. Tony Blair was probably the most committed of all to trying to get the NHS right. These people feel passionate about reform, and want to do the best they can by the British citizen. Over the last few years they have, quite bravely, taken on a vested interest in the NHS (particularly the reactionary part of the doctor community), and come up with an impressive policy agenda – driven, in particular, by the advisers to Number 10 and the Department of Health (Paul Corrigan and Simon Stevens). Despite being extremely well-intentioned, this group suffers from two problems:

- Too few of them have any experience of management. They have not had to deal with modern business, where managing change, because of the rigours of competition, is a core skill. What politicians and their advisers are good at is creating policy – and while, as I have argued, this is very necessary, in the absence of management skills to implement it, then policy will achieve very little.
- Despite their lack of management experience, the group does get involved in management. Whether it is launching yet another policy initiative, or reacting to the latest press report or to the latest questions in Parliament, or designing a new set of 'targets', there is a flood of 'directives' coming from the politicians and their advisers. Each of these directives, individually, usually makes sense, but they are not part of a coherent change programme: they sometimes conflict, and they always contribute to the torrent that overwhelms and distracts the frontline managers from getting on with their jobs.

Civil servants/senior NHS managers

There is a profound conservatism within the Civil Service. This is something that not only exists, but is also something in which they take pride.

They see their roles as smoothing things over rather than confronting them, and their objective as maintaining the status quo rather than bringing about change. Ken Livingstone, mayor of London, talks, regarding the transport sector, about the civil servants who 'manage decline gracefully'. It is difficult to think of a mindset less appropriate to bringing about the types of change and reform that the NHS needs. This is a broader issue than the NHS – it is the factor that is sabotaging public-sector reform generally. The public sector accounts for nearly 40 per cent of GDP and 20 per cent of UK employment. This 20 per cent of the UK workforce also owns 40 per cent of the 'pension commitment' and accounts for over 80 per cent of the days lost through strikes. Chronic waste and poor service to the public (a major feature of the NHS) is endemic within the Civil Service (from the deep incompetence that has resulted in the tax credit fiasco at Revenue and Customs, to the well-reported mess in the Home Office). It is almost universally the case that the people appointed to lead change in the NHS/Civil Service are civil servants. But it is difficult to understand how someone who has been brought up within the system, someone who is, by dint of being a career civil servant, responsible for (and complicit in) creating the situation that needs to be changed, can then be expected to have the drive, experience and broad perspective to be able to change it. Too many senior NHS managers – and senior civil servants more broadly – will mouth reform (to appease their reform-minded politician bosses), but will resist change.

Frontline NHS managers

These people have an unenviable job. They are the victims of a centralized bureaucracy. From the politicians, they get daily 'imperatives', which distract them from their longer-term objectives by forcing them to react to the latest 'fad'. From the senior civil servants/NHS managers, they get, at best, Stalinesque directives, and at worst meaningless, bureaucratic and poorly thought-through decisions. A common directive is the announcement of yet another reorganization. It is a feature of bureaucracies that regular reorganizations, which give the impression of 'change', are announced. This has been a central feature of 'change' within the NHS since the late 1990s – meaningless reorganizations that have ended up adding more waste in the form of additional administrative layers and bureaucratic processes, and high redundancy/reorganization costs. In a 2004 study on quality in the NHS by Leatherman and Sutherland[2] (which will be referred to further in Chapter 1), they remarked that 'A widely noted weakness of the Quality Agenda, as well as of the NHS itself, is its perennial reorganization. This is not just "around the edges" change; it is often large enough an overhaul to displace functions significantly, affect people by role changes and significantly shift operating budgets. In other words, disruptive and distracting changes are par for the course.'

Even if the NHS attracted the best managers in the world, this would be a hugely difficult environment in which to manage (a broader systemic diagnosis of the management challenge is described later). But, despite this, there are some very good managers in the NHS. However, in general, this malignant environment is bound to be unattractive to most good managers. As a result, poor management contributes to the dysfunctional organizational dynamics. I have been a manager in the private sector for around thirty years, and worked across the world in and with many organizations (including, of course, the public sector). The NHS, in terms of low management quality and dysfunctional organizational dynamics, is among the worst I have seen.

The challenge of change in the NHS is immense. The NHS is a highly complex 'system' characterized by, among other things, a very high public profile (it is the most 'cherished' institution in the country); a highly charged political context (as a consequence of its public profile); subject to ever-increasing demands from an ageing and increasingly demanding public; and employing disparate but highly organized and opinionated sub-groups (the public-sector unions, doctors and nurses – and, of course, politicians and civil servants). Anyone used to bringing about change in the private sector would admit that there is no more difficult challenge in the UK – perhaps in the world – than managing change in the NHS. The lack of a coherent and explicit change programme is even more damning in this context – and is itself evidence that the change process is not being managed coherently. The process of change in the private sector is the norm these days. The generic elements of change management are:

1. Construct a robust diagnosis of why change is required and what prevents change.
2. Describe a vision that will give meaning to the change process, and will provide a 'reason' to which people can orientate themselves when the going, inevitably, becomes tough and disorientating.

3. Break the old dysfunctional system dynamics by acting on the diagnosis with three or four well-placed, sustained and co-ordinated interventions.
4. Implement the new, functional dynamics, and through deliberate and planned communication, keep orientating people towards the vision.
5. Create a self-sustaining system whereby processes, motivations and rewards are constantly pointing the individual actors within the system to the objective of **patient value**.

None of these generic elements exists in the reform programme now under way in the NHS. Unless and until competent management do these five things, not only will real reform of the NHS be stillborn, but the chaos created by a random, unmanaged change process will potentially degrade the system even more than if nothing at all had been done in the first place. This would be a very sad heritage for Tony Blair and his colleagues, given their commitment to patient-centred reform. And it would be a disaster for the country.

A diagnosis of why change is required, and what prevents change

The first step is to make the case for change. The UK has some of the poorest health outcomes in the Organization for Economic Co-operation and Development (OECD). Cancer survival rates are among the lowest in the developed world, as shown in Figure I.4.

Since spending has been increased dramatically in recent years, real frontline improvement in care has been disappointing – too much of the money has been wasted. Although nurses and doctors continue to do the best by their patients day in and day out, they have never been more disillusioned with the system and its management (despite having received hefty pay increases since 2000). The case for change is overwhelming, but it has not been made coherently. Not only is the 'supply side' (the NHS system) underperforming, but also the 'demand side' pressures (citizen/consumer expectations and demands) are increasing. The population, traditionally content to 'leave it up to the doctor' is becoming better-educated about what constitutes good care, and furthermore, medical

Men   Women

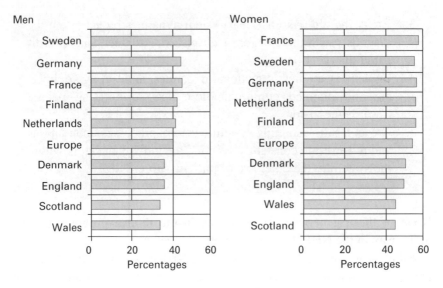

Source: Eurocare 3, *Health Service Journal*, June 2004.

Figure I.4   Five-year relative survival rates for men and women given a diagnosis in 1990–4

science is making available products such as the cancer-fighting drug Herceptin that can dramatically improve wellbeing. The underperforming NHS system combined with rising citizen/consumer expectations is a combustible mixture, giving ever greater urgency to the need for change. Chapter 1 of this book goes into the case for change in more detail.

Change cannot be a random process. There needs to be a good diagnosis of what has caused the situation that need to be changed. Too often, people say we should not waste time wondering how we got here – we should just get on with things and move forward; but this is a flawed approach. Without understanding how we got here, we shall not understand what it is that will prevent us from moving on. A good diagnosis is not only important in terms of directing management effort; it is also an essential ingredient of the change process itself. Unless the majority of participants in a system buy into the need for change and, just as importantly, buy into the diagnosis as to what is creating bad outcomes, then change is not going to occur. The fact is that the NHS is systemically dysfunctional, and poor management is at the core of its failure. A centralized bureaucracy, civil servants in the Department of Health, and politicians are sending out a daily flurry of directives, targets, reorganizations, new priorities, guidelines and decisions. This makes practical daily management out in the field extremely difficult. As a result, too many good managers give up and leave, and competent managers who can have a more rewarding life in the private sector are not attracted to the NHS (and, in many cases, are not even invited to join – the NHS is wary of, and unhelpful to, people from the private sector, or, as they call it, people from 'the dark side'). As a result, clinicians have a poor regard for NHS managers, and they are frustrated by operating in a poorly managed environment. Doctors are too often standing around when they want to be treating their patients: in one estimate, 30 per cent of patients who have an appointment at an acute hospital do not arrive – compared to 3 per cent in better-managed, private-sector facilities (treating comparable NHS patients); theatre capacity utilization in the private sector is about twice as efficient as in the NHS, and so on. These features create regular crises, which cause the civil servants and politicians to send out more directives, and the vicious circle is complete. And this system, despite being dysfunctional, is highly stable and difficult to penetrate. The fact that the NHS is in effect a monopoly means that poor performance remains trapped in the system – there are no competitive forces to allow the good performers to take over from the poor ones. Underperformance is 'trapped' within the system. This vicious circle is illustrated in Figure I.5.

The diagnosis of how the NHS got to where it is today, together with a deeper analysis of its dysfunctional dynamics, is the subject of Chapter 2.

A vision

In this vision for the NHS, there is detailed data, published and made available to the public as soon as it is produced, on the quality of clinical outcomes. These are not at the unhelpful level of a hospital, or even of a unit within a hospital (readmission rates, mortality rates and so on) but at the relevant level that shows which clinical teams produce which outcomes along a number of dimensions (survival rates, speed of return to work, complication rates and so on). These will have been defined and refined over the years by the clinicians themselves – within the regulatory framework constructed by the Healthcare Commission. They are risk-adjusted (obviously, outcomes will be worse for the aged or for those with other illnesses), and they are defined over the full cycle of care – they do

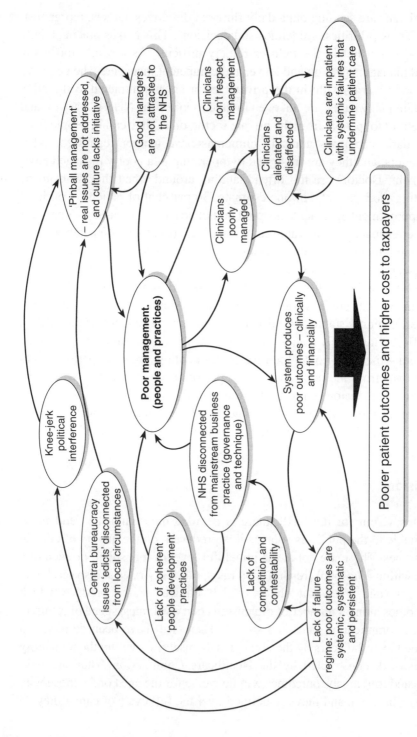

Figure I.5   The vicious circle of poor management

not define, for example, the single result of an operation, but look at the operation in the overall context of how a patient is treated for a particular condition. And these conditions are well defined. Cancer is too broad a category – even breast cancer is too broad a category: medical science has progressed to such an extent that we now know there are different types of breast cancer, with differing treatment regimes and differing outcome possibilities. This information on clinical outcomes is at the core of a patient-driven, highly responsive system (as will be described in more detail below). Its resolute focus is **patient value.**

The publication of this data, in itself, promotes better medical understanding of conditions. Clinicians have a much broader data set from which to understand what works and what does not, thus giving them access to a much broader experience set from which they can learn. Differential outcome data will have allowed clinicians to make hypotheses and to test them – and medical science has progressed as a result. Despite much talk in the NHS about evidence-based medicine, there is astonishingly little quality data. Without data clinicians and managers cannot make the right decisions, and they cannot learn.

In the early days, the publication of results will be shocking to people – it will show them how much difference there is in the quality of the clinical teams. To use an example from Professor Michael Porter's book *Redefining Healthcare* (the book is about the US system, but is very relevant also to the UK), there are 139 transplant facilities in the USA. This would, to a businessman, seem a very high figure. It is evidence of the way that healthcare, in the USA just as much as in the UK, has remained a local activity, and hence does not reap the advantages (to patients) of economies of scale and the experience curve. The best of these transplant facilities is excellent – and has a 100 per cent one-year survival rate: that is, every person who receives a transplanted organ at this facility survives for more than a year. But the worst facilities have a 1 per cent one-year survival rate! The idea that people would not travel to be treated by an excellent clinical team if that information were available to them is absurd.

Once customer-friendly data is published, people will realise (a) that huge variability in clinical outcomes exists; and (b) that choice is not an end in itself but rather a means to an end – it is the process whereby poor performance is rooted out, and better, safer clinical providers 'get the job'. This experience will finally quieten the people, mainly those who oppose reform, who say that patients do not want a choice – all they want is an excellent local hospital. Only the hardcore still will not accept that the only way to get an excellent local hospital is to allow providers to compete, based on outcome data, for the privilege of being chosen by patients/consumers/citizens. This is what is meant in this book by 'giving the system back to the patients and citizens of this country'.

In this vision, there will also be a huge improvement in the quality of economic data – the data that measures cost-effectiveness. This data is also poorly available in the NHS, making informed management process almost impossible. Some courses of treatment have better outcomes, but they are simply unaffordable. Tough trade-offs have to be made about where money can be deployed cost-effectively in the public good. These choices will be made by commissioners who, especially as they will be under public scrutiny, deploy data to show that public money is better spent on, say, Herceptin than on some other drug.

There is, in this vision, unrestrained competition. The best provider, measured by outcomes, has the job of providing the service. This is driven by a combination of high-quality commissioning (the 'dispensers' of public money will constantly assess who is doing well and who is doing badly, and if a clinical team is doing badly, then their service is put up for tender and those who can do a better job are brought in) and patient choice. The commissioners, if they are not quick to react to poor performance, will be disciplined by patients who, because of the availability of published data, have access to the information they need to choose which providers they want to use.

This 'unconstrained competition' will not mean a huge expansion of the private sector. Still, the vast majority of care will be provided by affiliated NHS institutions. What will happen, in this vision, is that the NHS Foundation Trusts will be 'let off the leash'. Those that have excellent clinical units will have competed for, and won, the right to take their expertise to other parts of the country. It is a nonsense that, for example, the Royal Brompton Hospital, world-renowned in treating respiratory disease, or Great Ormond Street Hospital, world famous for paediatric care, are not allowed to make their services available in Newcastle-upon-Tyne, or Liverpool, or wherever else they can demonstrate that they produce better results than the local clinical practitioners. The competitive revolution within the NHS will, ironically, be wrought from within the NHS itself. It has been an own-goal that the government has led on the role of the private sector in reforming the public sector. The private sector has an important role to play – quite simply, if a private-sector company can produce better health outcomes at a lower cost to taxpayers then it should be allowed to do so. But the private sector represents about 3 per cent of the total NHS spend, and the clinicians, who are the central engine of **patient value**, work the vast majority of their time in the NHS. Letting the Foundation Trusts, like the Royal Brompton, drive the competitive, patient-centred agenda would have been a much more defensible (and workable) strategy.

The government's policy agenda contains many of the initiatives that will contribute to this vision – but it needs to put **patient value**, and competition to increase **patient value**, at the heart of the reform programme. These two themes should be the 'maypole' around which all other policy initiatives dance. Not only will they provide conceptual coherence, they also provide a moral and ethical imperative. A central theme of this book is that the 'old' left and the public sector unions have betrayed the founding principles of the NHS: in their defence of their own privileges and in their authoritarianism, the 'old' left and the public-sector unions have become the 'new' right. The debate needs to move from ideology (state monopoly versus competition) to something much more objective and much more unarguably moral. This is **patient value**, and the role of competition in maximizing the objective of **patient value**. Arguments can be settled, one way or another, by determining, with data, which option or which provider will increase **patient value**.

This competitive revolution will take many of the lessons that have been learnt in other sectors and, finally, apply modern business strategies to healthcare. Activity in healthcare has suffered from being:

- *Too broad*, in that hospitals want to provide the full range of services. One of the attacks against Independent Sector Treatment Centres (ISTCs – the private-sector hospitals providing, mainly elective surgery to NHS patients) is that if you take away one or two activities from the local NHS Trust, then the whole hospital will suffer and eventually close. This is nonsense. We need to have 'focused factories' developing the scale and experience base on which they can build excellence. Far too many hospitals dabble in activities and specialities from which they gain no advantage when measured in terms of **patient value**. Their clinical outcomes are poor. And if patients knew the dangers, and were able to exercise choice, they would travel as far as was necessary to avoid them.

- *Too narrow*, in that the healthcare system is not organized around a full cycle of care for the patient. Most obviously, primary care and secondary care are separate, with poor communication between the two. And then there is sub-specialization (which is good in terms of scale and experience) but there are few integrating mechanisms. Pathology services, imaging activity, surgical interventions, physiotherapy and so on, create a 'pinball' experience for patients. We need depth of expertise, but also breadth of integration to produce coherent care pathways.
- *Too local*, in that everyone wants their local hospital. This is a major threat to patient safety. Study after study has shown the importance of scale and experience – the data shows that clinical services need to be consolidated in order to ensure patient safety.

Chapter 3 examines this vision in more detail, drawing heavily on the excellent work that Professor Michael Porter has done in the USA.

Breaking the vicious circle

The type of dynamics illustrated in Figure I.5 is astonishingly difficult to break. By definition, the various parts are self-supporting. Trying to attack one of them – clinical disengagement, for example, or centralized bureaucracy – will fail because it will be overwhelmed by the power of the rest of the 'system'.

Experience in change in the private sector shows that such powerful dynamics can only be broken if the 'system' is perforated at a number of points – and in a programmed, coherent and systematic way. The chart below shows the three major points where the system needs to be broken – and the imperatives are to (1) decentralize/de-bureaucratize/depoliticize; (2) extend and strengthen demand-side mechanisms; and (3) release the power of unrestrained competition. A fourth imperative is to bring in non-NHS/Civil Service management in critical senior positions, and progressively throughout the organization, in order to drive this change process forward. See Figure I.6.

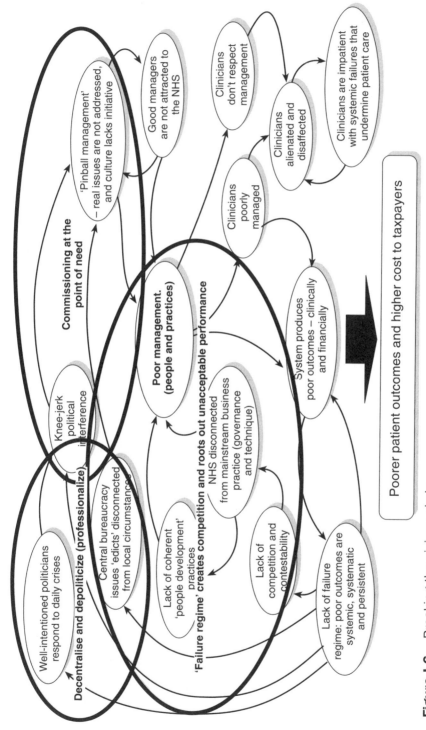

Figure I.6 Breaking the vicious circle

1. Decentralize/de-bureaucratize/depoliticize

A mistake that the private sector makes all too often, and keeps rediscovering – organizations only work well when you push decision-making and responsibility as close to the patient/consumer as possible. And that responsibility has to be based only on results, not on compliance with orders. The NHS is in urgent need of decentralization. The new NHS Strategic Health Authority (SHA) chief executives have to become accountable and responsible for the outcomes they produce. And they have to drive that accountability right down to the frontline unit management. A large part of the waste that has been created over the past few years is caused by this lack of accountability. A number of hospital managers, for example, faced with the 'threat' of competition from the private sector (in the form of Independent Sector Treatment Centres) decided to pre-empt this by building their own facilities. Diagnostic Treatment Centres – mini-hospitals – sprang up throughout the country. Figure I.6 shows the extent of NHS extravagance.

Too many now lie idle, because they were never really needed (physical capacity was never the problem – management of capacity was the issue), and the people who put them up knew that they would not be held accountable for the waste of public money. In the private sector, such bad decisions would result in the manager being fired – or, indeed, if the mistakes were big enough, then the whole organization would collapse. There are no second chances in the private sector.

A corollary to this decentralization is that the Department of Health should be considerably downsized – if not closed completely. The experience of centralized bureaucracies around the world – from the Stalinist Kremlin to the NHS itself – is that the central office (the HQ), undisciplined by competition, grows. The Department of Health would show little loss of usefulness if it were reduced to 20 per cent of what it is now, or even disbanded completely. This is not only a cost saving in its own right (the monies would be redeployed to clinical care), but the system effects would be hugely beneficial. It is not possible to have responsible and accountable managers on the ground if they are being second-guessed and ordered around by a central office.

Bureaucracies have some very distinctive characteristics, and these are clearly evident in the NHS. They are driven by centralized directives, they mistake reorganization for real change, they are insular, inward-looking and suspicious of outsiders, they administer rather than manage, and lack

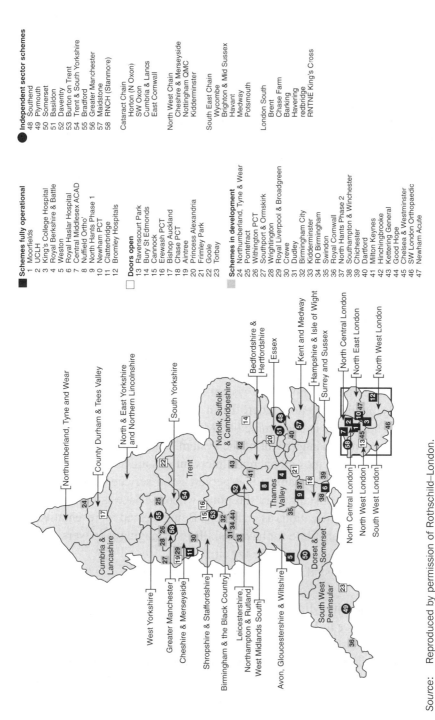

Schemes fully operational
1 Moorfields
2 UCLH
3 King's College Hospital
4 Royal Berkshire & Battle
5 Weston
6 Royal Haslar Hospital
7 Central Middlesex ACAD
8 Nuffield Ortho'
9 North Hants Phase 1
10 Newham PCT
11 Clatterbridge
12 Bromley Hospitals

Doors open
13 Ravenscourt Park
14 Bury St Edmonds
15 Cannock
16 Erewash PCT
17 Bishop Auckland
18 Chase PCT
19 Aintree
20 Princess Alexandra
21 Frimley Park
22 Goole
23 Torbay

Schemes in development
24 Northumberland, Tyne & Wear
25 Pontefract
26 Withington PCT
27 Southport & Ormskirk
28 Wrightington
29 Royal Liverpool & Broadgreen
30 Crewe
31 Dudley
32 Birmingham City
33 Kidderminster
34 RO Birmingham
35 Swindon
36 Royal Cornwall
37 North Hants Phase 2
38 Southampton & Winchester
39 Chichester
40 Dartford
41 Milton Keynes
42 Hinchingbrooke
43 Kettering General
44 Good Hope
45 Chelsea & Westminster
46 SW London Orthopaedic
47 Newham Acute

Independent sector schemes
48 Southend
49 Plymouth
50 Somerset
51 Basildon
52 Daventry
53 Burton on Trent
54 Trent & South Yorkshire
55 Bradford
56 Greater Manchester
57 Maidstone
58 RNCH (Stanmore)

Cataract Chain
Horton (N Oxon)
SW Oxon
Cumbria & Lancs
East Cornwall

North West Chain
Cheshire & Merseyside
Nottingham QMC
Kidderminster

South East Chain
Wycombe
Brighton & Mid Sussex
Havant
Medway
Portsmouth

London South
Brent
Chase Farm
Barking
Havering
redbridge
RNTNE King's Cross

Source: Reproduced by permission of Rothschild–London.

Figure I.7 Expansion of NHS capacity

accountability for results – promotion is based on 'keeping your nose clean' and 'politicking'. There are, of course, private-sector bureaucracies also – but the number of them has declined considerably, since many markets have either been deregulated (such as the traditionally cosy 'City' of London prior to the 'Big Bang' in the mid-1980s) or buffeted by changing global conditions (such as in the oil and gas industries, where traditional private-sector bureaucracies, such as Shell, are being shaken out of their torpor).

Management practice in bureaucracies is poor. And this poverty of management practice is evident in the NHS. Human resources (HR) systems (such as objective-setting, performance reviews and so on) are poor or non-existent. Data on which to make good decisions is, at best, inconsistent and partial (and this, in turn, is a sign that poor management has failed to install systems that can calculate important metrics, which in turn are a fundamental tool of competent management), and implementation is poor. Even basic management practices – such as running a good meeting, or even turning up on time – are poor in the NHS. Management at all levels has to be held accountable for putting these things right. And if they fail, then they should, after 'due process', be fired – and when they are fired, they should not get a large redundancy cheque at the taxpayer's expense.

These are just some of the elements of a consistent programme that is required to de-bureaucratize the system.

Finally, in this category, there is an urgent need to depoliticize the service. The service is undermined by Ministers of State getting involved in the day-to-day management of the system. Their well-intentioned, but random (and sometimes incoherent) interventions are a major contributor to the dysfunctional dynamics that pervert good service to patients. Not only are they too distant from the point where service is delivered, but they have few qualifications as managers. Being elected representatives of the people is no substitute for having skills in managing taxpayers' money to deliver a high-quality service for citizens.

Aneurin Bevan said, when he launched the NHS:

After 5 July the Minister of Health will be the whipping boy for the Health Service in Parliament. Every time a maid kicks over a bucket of slops in a ward an agonised wail will go through Whitehall. After the new service is introduced there will be a cacophony of complaints. The newspapers will be full of them. For a while, it will appear that everything is going wrong. As a matter of fact, everything will be going right.[3]

This quote is well known, and people use it to justify the inevitable politicization of the process. But many people do not know that Bevan went on to say that this would only last for a few weeks or months, and then people would start fixing their problems locally. He got a lot of things right, but not this one – sixty years later, the ringing of the 'bucket of slops' is still creating a cacophony in Westminster, which in turn generates knee-jerk responses. This has to stop.

The government should be responsible for making sure that taxpayers' money is well spent, but it should *not* be responsible for managing the organization that spends it. We need to create more professional/clinical bodies that make decisions based on good managerial and, in particular, clinical criteria. The formation of the National Institute for Clinical Excellence (NICE) has, on the whole, been a good innovation, but we need to extend this success to include other areas of decision-making. We have, for example, far too many hospitals throughout the country. Medical research shows that these services have to be consolidated – *in the interests of patients*. Scale and experience are crucial drivers of successful clinical outcomes. Keeping open the local hospital might make a great political rallying-cry, but it threatens patient safety. Some people claim that the political bandwagon results in hospitals in marginal seats being kept open (ironically, endangering the constituents) and hospitals in 'opposition' seats are closed (again, ironically, benefiting the local community). If this happens, and one hopes it does not, it is nonsense. Either way, we should have a professional body that gives mature and thoughtful managerial and clinical judgements on decisions of this sort. This is an important way, also, of getting clinicians back to the heart of our health service.

Politicians are torn between the wish to rid themselves of the day-to-day grind that their close involvement in the service creates for them, and on the other hand, the 'tradition' (to repeat here, *not* one that Bevan wanted to set up) of Ministers of State having close involvement and day-to-day accountability. On the other hand, there might be a sense of power that Ministers feel when they can have such direct control over the service. But this megalomania has to be resisted – politicians need to distance themselves increasingly from the management of the NHS – otherwise they will, knowingly or not, contribute to the system's poor performance.

2. Extend and strengthen demand-side mechanisms

There are four key demand-side mechanisms that are required to move change and service improvement forward.

The first is the publication and dissemination of *clinical outcomes*, as a precursor to a central focus on **patient value**. This was the core part of the 'vision' outlined earlier, and of the moral imperative, again outlined earlier; it will be dealt with further in Chapter 3. The government is right to push the concept of patient choice, but it was an 'own goal' to do so before there was data showing how much clinical outcomes differ between different clinical teams (or, indeed, the bad – even fatal – clinical consequences of having to wait a long time for NHS treatment), and therefore demonstrating how important is the exercise of choice.

Patient choice is a key feature of reform, and is the second demand-side mechanism. There is no evidence anywhere in the world that complex systems can be reformed by supply-side change only. The NHS has to be held accountable to both the patient and the taxpayer; and the government needs to recover from its 'own goal'. The first thing that needs to be done is to force the publication of outcome data – which is still extremely difficult to access within the NHS, and, too often, does not exist at all – and then people would understand what choice is all about. In fact, the clamour for it will be irresistible, and will overwhelm the resistance to choice from some parts of the medical community, from the public sector unions and from the 'old' left. As it is, patients do not really have the data on which to make choice, therefore they are puzzled about the benefits of choice (too often assuming that doctors are perfect, and that outcomes are the same across the country), and so the doctors opposed to reform and unions can claim that patients do not really want it.

The third demand-side mechanism is effective *commissioning*. Again, this is an own goal by the government. An important criticism of the government's policy agenda is that it has focused too much on supply-side policies (because they do not have any experience of how to bring about change within an organization, and the importance of 'pulling through reform' from the demand side). To be fair to the government, they have realized this error and commissioning is now high on their reform agenda. Commissioning is often thought of as contracting for services. It is that, but contracting is only one small part of it. Real commissioning is a crucial driver of the 'new' system. The process of commissioning, in the sense of the commissioners being the 'guarantors' that taxpayers money is being spent on **patient value** as effectively as possible, is as follows:

- *Determining the health needs of a region.* Healthcare needs in inner city areas are likely to be very different from those in suburban and rural areas. Although there will always be national healthcare objectives, one size never fits all, and each region will need to fine-tune its priorities according to its own definition of **patient value**, which will be determined by a variety of factors – social class, poverty, age profile, ethnicity and so on. This would entail building an epidemiological map for each region. Such data exists in some cases – but it is incomplete, inconsistent, and not widely distributed.
- *Designing and adopting care pathways* for discrete medical conditions, and introducing, where appropriate, chronic disease management. As Michael Porter's new research in the USA shows, continuity of care over the disease/treatment cycle will produce better health outcomes: 'The more experience physicians and teams have in treating patients with a particular disease or condition, the more likely they are to create better outcomes – and, ultimately lower costs. By performing particular procedures over and over, teams increase their learning opportunities and thereby reduce mortality rates'.[4] This perspective from the patient's point of view – instead of the supply-side point of view – will radically change the way our healthcare system is designed. In particular, it will break down the ridiculous divide between primary and secondary care which in the UK institutionalizes fragmented patient care.
- *Combining the epidemiological map with the care pathways* to produce a 'Better Health Outcomes Model' that describes how the specific health needs of a region can be met and outcomes improved.
- *Defining the objective of the regional healthcare economy* and allocating scarce resources against explicit trade-offs so that the optimal solution is reached. The first task is to define the 'objective function', drawing the boundary constraints, such as resources, and identifying the optimal solution.
- *Commissioning the best provider*, public, private or voluntary sector to deliver the solution. The only criterion, from a patient's

point of view, is which provider can produce the best outcome (at the most efficient cost to taxpayers).

- *Performance-managing the provider* and, if necessary, replacing poor performers. As part of this process, commissioners collect the data that will allow reassessment and refinement of the 'Better Health Outcomes Model'. And this completes the virtuous circle as the commissioners learn more about the epidemiology of their region, and, crucially, learn what works and what does not work – it now informs the process of *determining the health needs of a region* (see Figure I.8).

This commissioning process is a never-ending cycle. The commissioners would be, in effect, the 'keepers' of the public good: but this function should not (as will be argued in the next section) be confused with the

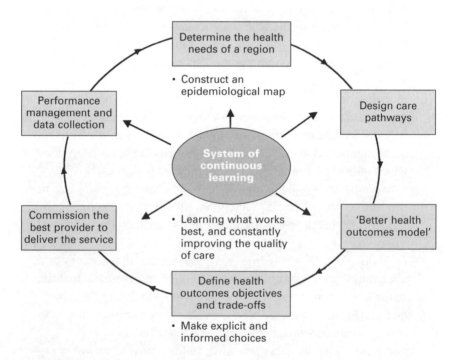

Figure I.8   The virtuous circle of commissioning

need to actually provide the care. The monopoly NHS has fudged the distinction between the commissioning and provider function for many years – the distinction has to be clear, in the public good.

The fourth key issue is reform of *primary healthcare*. Although primary care costs much less money than secondary care, it is where 80 per cent of the patients' experience of the NHS happens. Moreover, because of our system of channelling all patients through the GP 'gate-keeper', this is the crucial point where much important diagnosis takes place. Publication of results in this sector is fiercely opposed on the basis of it 'being too difficult'. This is nonsense; general practices should be judged on their results like everyone else. Unsurprisingly, reform of primary healthcare is urgent. It has, up to now, been low on the government's priority list, but the government is now beginning to turn its attention to reform in this part of the system.

Chapter 4 will, in the broader context of the total reform programme, look specifically at reform in primary healthcare. Again, key themes are transparency of outcomes, better information for patients/citizens, and unrestrained competition, so that the system works for the patient and not for the providers.

3.   Release the power of unrestrained competition

The principle here is very clear and simple – the *best* provider should provide the public service – irrespective of whether it is a public-sector, private-sector or voluntary organization. This concept is deeply threatening to, and passionately opposed by, the monopoly NHS (and more broadly by the monopoly public sector). But the implications of opposing it are very serious. For those who advocate that only the public-sector monopoly should be allowed to provide the service,and (as is most often the case) the public-sector body, for the very reason that it is uncompetitive, produces worse clinical outcomes at a higher cost to taxpayers, then the defenders of the NHS monopoly are, in effect, damaging the health of UK patients, and stealing from UK taxpayers.

As was argued above, the irony is that the private sector will probably play quite a small part in achieving the vision outlined. The private sector is a tiny part of the overall UK healthcare system – accounting for about 3 per cent of the NHS budget (many people, reading the newspaper headlines and the hysteria around 'privatization' might be surprised at this figure). The bulk of competition in the NHS will be driven by the clinical teams within Foundation Trusts (and the majority of NHS acute care hospitals will become Foundation Trusts over the next few years). We must create a system whereby excellent units such as the Royal Brompton or Great Ormond Street – if they can prove their excellence in terms of **patient value** – are allowed to become regional and then national organizations, competing against, and replacing, worse-performing NHS units elsewhere in the country. Why should the people of, say, Newcastle or Liverpool, not have the same quality of care in cardiovascular disease management as the people of Chelsea?

Unless there is competition to ensure that the patient's interests are best served, then we shall have an underperforming system – that will fail both patients and taxpayers – for generations to come. The enemy is not the public sector *per se*, it is monopoly abuse of power, and the answer is not private-sector involvement as such; it is the introduction of competition so that **patient value** becomes the overriding objective of the National Health Service.

There has been much criticism of the government's introduction of a tariff to measure the cost that a procedure incurs. That the monopoly NHS should oppose the idea that we need to know how much a procedure costs so that we can understand who is doing a procedure more cheaply (that is, spending taxpayers' money more wisely) is a testament to just how insular, defensive, and unconcerned (about both patients' and taxpayers' rights) it is. Of course, the tariff (or PbR – payment by results) needs to be refined to accommodate cost/benefit trade-offs. It might cost more to do a certain procedure, but the patient might live longer/suffer less pain/have a lower chance of incurring costs through, for example, readmission or the application of more expensive drugs. The PbR system has, over time, to become sophisticated enough to make these trade-offs transparent, but there is no doubt that we need to access, understand and act (managerially) on the data. Competition will mean that the most appropriate cost/benefit trade-offs are made.

Competition is a crucial aspect of reform. The government has generally been moving along the right road here. But too often, and in particular in Patricia Hewitt's early days as Secretary of State, there was equivocation about how much competition would be introduced – semantic hair-splitting with words such as 'contestability' were used to suggest that there would be transparency, but not really competition in any normal sense. There was denial that the healthcare system is a market. This fuzzy thinking has to stop – and it is reassuring that Hewitt has recently said that there should be no constraints to private sector involvement if patient interests are served. We need to introduce competition in the interest of ensuring a focus on the moral imperative of **patient value**, and we need to introduce market dynamics – to do what a market does: make sure, through competition, that scarce resources are used efficiently in order to satisfy patient (consumer) needs.

There is no evidence anywhere in the world that patient/consumer interests can be served by any system other than producers competing to deliver the best service at the best cost.

4. Bring in new senior management

There has been no situation in the UK – or anywhere else in the world, in fact – where the people who have been a part of a dysfunctional system have been able to change the system they helped to create. They have built their careers by being successful in the current system – and even if they knew anything different – which they cannot because they are career NHS/Civil Service managers – then their skills are appropriate to the old world, not the new. At best, incumbent managers are complicit in the mess of the NHS, and at worst are architects of it. Therefore, in order to change the NHS, new external management is required. The number of managers recruited from outside the traditional ranks of the NHS does not have to be large, and it is important that the new, external, management mobilizes the bulk of the existing NHS management to change (the task would be impossible without taking the bulk of the incumbents along), but it does have to be the most senior management posts that are held by new managers with private-sector experience – these are the managers who have the benefit of seeing things from the outside, are not hidebound by conforming to 'the way things are done around here', and have experience of how to change things.

These four imperatives will be discussed in more detail in Chapter 4.

Implementing the new, functional dynamics

A key theme in this book is that the core problem with reform in the NHS is that incumbent senior management, politicians or civil servants are incapable of managing a change programme of this magnitude, complexity and importance. Policy, it has been argued, is generally acceptable; funding is generous. The big problem is the organization and the management, and this is nowhere more crucial than in the implementation of reform. Too much of NHS management, 'at the coal-face', is not up to the task – it is, generally, philosophically opposed to reform (its rhetoric is about the iniquities of competition and the 'private sector', but its underlying motivation is about protecting its rights and lack of accountability). The list of implementation 'must dos' is not rocket science – they are common practice in the competitive private sector. However, they are absent from management practice in the public sector. The 'golden rules' of implementation are as follows:

- Create a *vision* that people can buy into and orientate themselves towards. The vision was sketched out earlier, and will be outlined more fully in Chapter 3. No compelling vision exists currently in the government's change programme.
- Get high quality *data* and act on it. Quality data is often just not there in much of the NHS. But even if the data *is* there – and the enquiry into the Bristol Royal Infirmary tragedy says that, in that case, the data was sometimes available but not used – there are no modern management information systems that turn the raw data into useful management information, and there is no system of accountability that forces managers to act on the information. There is almost a pride in the fact that things are too fast-moving to be able to collect and act on high-quality data – there is a sort of heroism within the NHS about managing by the 'seat of the pants'. Healthcare will not be allocated to the right place, and money will not be well spent unless high-quality data – about outcomes, costs, labour utilization and so on is easily available to management, and unless management is required to act on it.
- Make everyone, at all levels, *accountable* for delivering high-quality care at the most efficient cost. Such accountability is at best intermittent in the NHS. Public money is wasted, poor decisions are made, management is either constrained by the system or just not good enough – and no one pays the price.
- As I have argued, the NHS and the UK healthcare system is highly complex. New initiatives/policies have to be refined before they are rolled out nationwide – there is a need for *play-testing and piloting* to see if they work, and to learn from the successes and failures. This is too rarely done in the NHS. Partly this is

because, as described earlier, the politicians feel comfortable formulating and announcing policy – they think the formulation and announcement will make it happen; so they 'fire and forget'. But the system is (a) not managed, because of the poor quality of NHS management; and (b) even if the management was brilliant, no one can have the foresight to understand what the implications of a new policy will be in this complex healthcare system.

- *Make people decisions bravely and early.* In a change programme as far-reaching as the one the NHS needs, it is vital that senior managers decide early on who is (a) on board with the reform programme; and (b) competent enough to be a driver and manager of change. All organizations, private but especially public, tend to put up with poor performance longer than they should. Often, it is speciously justified in terms of 'compassion' or in the hope that 'people will improve'. These platitudes will seriously undermine a change programme. Without good people in place, reform is going to stutter forward – at best. The NHS not only has below-average management quality, but it also tends not to deal with the problem. This is a major behavioural change the NHS has to make.

- *Make decisions and manage meetings* Again, this management skill is not always as it should be in the private sector, but it is immeasurably worse in the public sector. Unwieldy Boards, bureaucratic processes and, most fundamentally, the absence of good information, all contribute to poor-quality decision-making, chronic planning blight, and the propensity towards inaction.

- In a change programme, it is important to *keep the momentum going*, and not be diverted by the people who scream that things need to slow down. There will be fewer of these screams in a well-managed change process, employing the techniques outlined above, but there will always be calls by those people whose inter-ests are threatened by change, or who are generally being pushed outside their 'comfort zone' to try to stop change. Of course, if they are allowed to succeed, then change will inevitably stall. There are a lot of these screams occurring in the NHS – partly because the change programme is not being well managed, but partly, too, because there are self-interested or ideological oppo-nents to the reform programme, and they must be stared down. Of course, senior management has to be sensitive to the need, at

times, to change gear – either up or down. Certainly, given how
poorly the change programme is being managed and communi-
cated, there is a need at this time to put in place a more coherent
programme, and it is likely that some aspects of reform do need
to be 'triaged'.
* *Analyse the behavioural and cultural barriers to change.* Even
  good managers tend to be more comfortable dealing with hard
  economic data than with the 'soft' facts of behaviour and culture.
  The type of system diagnosis that is at the core of this book is
  quite rare even in the private sector. But, especially in a culturally
  'rich' (that is, opinionated) and, often, divisive environment like
  the NHS, a good behavioural and cultural diagnosis is essential.

What all of this comes down to, again, is the need for competent management; experienced in managing the process of change.

Creating a self-sustaining system (and building the country's wealth in the process)

Managerial best practice, as outlined above, is not, however, enough in the
medium and long term. It is necessary in the short term to manage better
the centralized bureaucracy (and, as has been argued above, there is vast
scope for better management). But this is only a short-term requirement –
the underlying problem is the centralized bureaucracy itself. Senior civil
servant/NHS management has to make itself obsolete. This is patently not
something that the Civil Service mentality can contemplate – its mindset
is to create bureaucracy so it can justify its existence. What senior
managers should be doing is creating a healthcare economy that, like any
economy, has the following characteristics:

* *A value objective.* This has to be **patient value**. This is the equivalent of 'prices' in mainstream economic markets. This, as in any
  market, needs to be transparent and available to the public – who
  are, uniquely, both the providers of funds for this economy, and
  the consumers of its service.

- *Transparency of costs within individual units.* This is essential, so that the efficient survive and the inefficient (those wasting taxpayers' money) are ejected from the market.
- *Patient choice* is not an end in itself, but when patients have information (on both cost and value), then they are the mechanism that will ensure the system becomes self-sustaining. In terms of 'classical economics', their exercise of choice is the 'invisible hand' that makes the market work day-by-day – but only if . . .
- . . . there is *unrestrained competition* such that the patient's exercise of choice does ensure that those organizations/units that enhance **patient value** are rewarded, and grow, and those that destroy **patient value** exit the market.
- *Commissioners are the market-makers.* They are the mechanism whereby monopolies are prevented from developing. They build up experience in defining health needs, and they are the market guardians who ensure that the patient remains at the centre of the system – and that we do not see a slide back to monopoly abuse of citizens.
- *The computer system* that the NHS is implementing is a crucial part of the process. 'Connecting for Health' will provide the information and transparency that is needed to put **patient value** at the centre of the UK healthcare system. The IT project is largely well conceived – but the priority should not have been patient choice (especially in the context of an absence of information on which consumers can base their right to choose); it should have been something that, in the first instance, the users (doctors) valued, which would have been consolidating patient notes and images. In this sense, the problem is that it is being poorly implemented. The golden rule in any IT project is to involve the users fully. The users in this case are the doctors. Not only were they not included, but the managers of the project took a very public pride in excluding them – saying that their exclusion was crucial to getting things under way. Predictably, the doctors have undermined the system. None the less, although there will be a resulting cost and delay, the system (or at least a version of it) looks as if it will come into being – and will become a vital enabler of the overall system reform that is advocated in this book.

> • Finally, like any market, there is *a need for tight regulation*. In terms of ensuring that the market works, and that market failure is quickly fixed by market entry, then the commissioners undertake this role. They need to operate within a broader regulatory framework – perhaps provided by an evolution of the role of the Foundation Trusts' regulatory body, Monitor, under its Chief Executive, Bill Moyes. The guardians of **patient value**, in terms of ensuring the quality of data produced and ensuring its wide circulation, should be a body like the Healthcare Commission.

These are the mechanisms that the change programme needs to introduce, and the mechanisms that will make the economy become self-sustaining. At the microeconomic level the key drivers of this are transparency of outcomes and unrestrained competition – these are reforms that will create an unstoppable momentum. Once citizens become familiar with the availability of information, and once they see that their choices can really create ongoing improvements, then the process of making the system patient-centred will become inexorable. The NHS change programme has to recognise that the objective is not just to change the organizational dynamics and root out obsolete/incompetent management practices within the NHS – but rather to create a 'service economy'. The design of this economy has to put in place self-supporting mechanisms, 'invisible hands', that make the system live, day-by-day. Top-down 'command and control', a Stalinist 'planned economy' has not, and will not, work.

The design principles required for this type of transformation will not be found only in microeconomic theory, but also in macroeconomic theory. The closest parallel is the transformation that the East European economies have gone through (with dramatic improvements, incidentally, in the standard of living of their inhabitants) since the end of communist rule in 1989.

As in Eastern Europe in 1989, so now in the NHS we need new leaders. A major theme of this book is the inappropriateness of Civil Service/traditional NHS management. But new leaders and new organizations are needed throughout the system:

> • Union resistance to productive change has to be broken – wilfully or otherwise, their actions are profoundly opposed to

patient value and the efficient spending of taxpayers' money. This applies most strongly to Unison and to the 'old left' of the British Medical Association (BMA). The Royal College of Nursing (RCN) has, traditionally, been more of a professional rather than a protectionist, self-interested body, but its treatment of Patricia Hewitt at its summer 2006 conference creates the concern that it is moving towards being an anti-competitive and anti-efficiency ideology.

- The clinicians – doctors in particular – are crucial to the success of the UK's future healthcare economy. New leaders there need to embrace the concept of **patient value**, the need for transparency of outcomes, and the need for competition so that the best doctors and clinical teams are able to take their skill and expertise to places where others are failing.
- The Foundation Trusts need to be 'let off the leash'. They will be the drivers of competition – it is they who will 'animate' a patient-orientated system. Some may evolve into for-profit organizations (often through joint ventures (JVs) with private-sector companies), but many will remain as not-for-profit organizations. And that is fine – there is no ideology in this book about private versus public sector. The only criterion for who gets the privilege of serving patients, is which organization does it the best.

Alongside this macroeconomic perspective, there is also a national competitiveness agenda. Not only has the NHS failed patients, but it has also had an impact on our national wealth. A vibrant healthcare economy in the UK – the type we had some decades ago when the NHS was one of the most respected healthcare systems in the world – earns money for the country by attracting paying patients from around the world, by attracting people who want to train in our healthcare sector and, most importantly, by creating competitive healthcare and pharmaceutical companies that both employ people in the UK, and repatriate international earnings. Chapter 5 looks at this international competitiveness perspective, and, taking the example of North West London, postulates a theory of what needs to happen to enable the UK to regain its position as world leader in healthcare.

The rest of this book is organized as follows:

Chapter 1: Although clinicians are dedicated to the welfare of their patients, they labour in a system that lets them down – a system in which waste is endemic, and in which poor organizational dynamics and poor management cause the system to underperform chronically. This chapter makes the case that the need for change is overwhelming.

Chapter 2: Without an explicit diagnosis of what is wrong with the NHS, a diagnosis that directs a change programme, then reform will go nowhere. This chapter expands on the diagnosis of what is wrong with the NHS – on the poor organizational dynamics and poor management. It charts the path of how the NHS got to where it is now.

Chapter 3: The core of the vision is: a focus on **patient value** (increasing the quality of patient outcomes over a full cycle of care, at the best cost); transparency of outcome data; and unrestrained competition to increase **patient value**. This chapter goes into more detail on this topic.

Chapter 4: Although the NHS is going through a massive change, there is no coherent change programme in place. This chapter outlines the elements of such a change programme.

Chapter 5: A crucial element of a change programme is an understanding of what is required to make the process of improvement self-sustaining. In this case, the elements that will create self-sustaining change are the transparency of patient outcomes, and the rights of patients to exercise choice in seeking out the providers who can give them the best outcomes. These need to be set in a broader context of a system that will effortlessly direct participants to do the right things. This chapter looks in more detail at this process, but it also looks at how we can get into a virtuous circle whereby our improving healthcare system also contributes to the economic wealth of the country by restoring the UK's position as a world leader in biomedical science.

In summary, this book argues that an even stronger reform process is required if the NHS is to be saved. Bevan said in 1948, 'We shall of course find from time to time that alterations and adjustments have to be made. We are not ridden by doctrine; we are a nation very largely of visionary empiricists, able to adjust things where necessary, and between us we shall have a standard of health service that will be the envy and admiration of the world.'[5]

Only by implementing the reforms outlined in this book shall we be able to rescue the NHS from those who are 'ridden by doctrine', and who have been the architects of a UK health service that is anything but the envy and admiration of the world. We have to drive through reform in order to honour the great achievement of Aneurin Bevan.

Footnote

Before the remaining chapters go into more detail, it is important to make the point of just what a time bomb is this issue of healthcare. The UK healthcare consumer has traditionally been hugely compliant and patient. Traditional respect for, and love of, the NHS persists. The abuses that go on – from Bristol Royal Infirmary to the waste of taxpayers' money – are tolerated in the public's treatment of the NHS in a way that, if this was the way their mortgage lenders, their supermarkets or their travel agents, or anybody else, treated them, they would be hopping mad. But this is going to change. The UK citizen is a 1950s grateful consumer when it comes to the NHS, but is a twenty-first century, demanding customer when it comes to everything else that they pay for. This is going to change over the next few years – citizens are going to become angry. And their anger is going to coincide with scientific progress that is going to make highly effective, but high-cost, drugs available to people – *to keep them alive*. In a system of waste and underachievement, this is going to increase the citizens' anger. Figures I.9 and I.10 demonstrate the increasing demand for healthcare spending – and these should be viewed in the

Effect of ageing, cancer, heart disease, medical negligence/obesity, family support, NHS pension/staff costs and public expectation

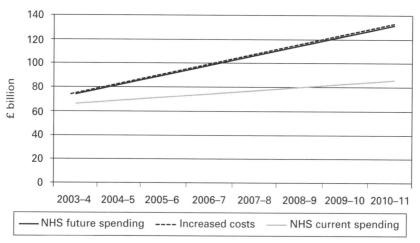

Source: Western Provident Association health insurers, http://www.wpa.org.uk/.

Figure I.9 NHS future spending versus current spending

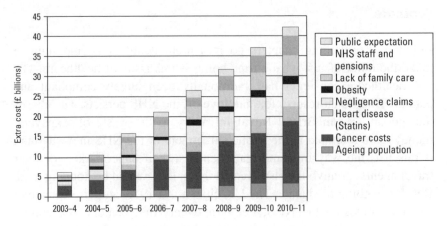

Source: Western Provident Association health insurers, http://www.wpa.org.uk.

Figure I.10   Breakdown of additional spend

context of the waste that current organizational dysfunction and poor
management creates – and also demonstrate that the current system will
reach breaking point in the near future unless reforms are accelerated.

The topic of healthcare funding is not one that I address in this book.
In the next few years, any supplementary funding regime above taxation
is very unlikely. The Labour government is committed to a tax-funded
system, and the Conservatives have also recently committed themselves
to this. Moreover, if the reforms outlined in this book are executed, there
is a huge amount of waste that can be taken out of the system. One of the
attractions of the focus on **patient value** is that the cost of more integrated
treatment of patients over a full cycle of care is likely to be less expensive
than the episodic, uncoordinated interventions that currently occur.

However, the inexorable rise in demand and the inevitable limits of
citizens' willingness to pay ever more taxes is going to bring this topic to
the forefront in the next few years.

1
The case for change

Key points

1   Much has been achieved by the Labour government since 1997.
2   Because of a lack of attention to dysfunctional organizational dynamics and poor NHS management, too much of the extra spending has been wasted.
3   The UK still compares poorly with other developed nations in terms of health outcomes.
4   The recommendations from the Bristol enquiry have still not been implemented adequately, and point to persistent management failings.

Much has been achieved by the Labour government since 1997

The Labour government insisted it inherited a problem when it was elected in 1997. Successive governments had filed the NHS in the 'too difficult (and too thankless)' category. Since 1997, the Labour government has resolutely addressed two of the three problems afflicting the NHS: they have put more money into it, and they have formulated sensible policy.

OECD statistics[1] put into perspective the position of the NHS in comparison with other European countries (see Table 1.1). In 1993, health expenditure per capita in the UK was lower than in all of the main European countries except Spain and Poland. Since 1997, however, the UK has had the fastest-rising expenditure on healthcare. But by 2003, despite the fact that health expenditure per capita had nearly doubled, the UK still lagged behind France, the Netherlands, Sweden and Switzerland, and was on a par with Italy and Austria.

Although at the time of writing the UK spends 7.7 per cent of GDP on

Table 1.1 UK health expenditure compared with other European countries

	Total expenditure as percentage of GDP		Public expenditure as percentage of total expenditure on health		Average growth rate	Health expenditure per capita US$ PPP	
	2003	1993	2003	1993	1998–2003	2003	1993
Austria	7.6	7.8	69.2	74.2	1.8	2280	1669
France	10.1	9.4	76.3	76.5	3.5	2903	1878
Germany	11.1	9.9	78.2	80.2	1.8	2996	1988
Poland	6.0	5.9	72.4	73.8	3.0	677	378
Spain	7.7	7.5	72.1	76.6	2.6	1835	1089
Sweden	9.2	8.6	85.3	87.4	5.4	2594	1644
Switzerland	11.5	9.4	58.5	54.3	2.8	3781	2401
UK	7.7	6.9	83.4	85.1	5.7	2231	2311

Source: OECD (2005) *Health Data.*

health, this figure is still lower than Germany, France, Italy, Spain, Sweden and Switzerland. This says two things – the UK government has made a real commitment to increasing the spending on healthcare, but it is a moving target as other countries also increase their spending.

Table 1.2 shows that the UK has made progress, but is still behind other major European countries with respect to practising physicians and diagnostics; the UK still has the lowest number of physicians and surgeons per head of population, and it has a substantially lower number of Magnetic Resonance Imaging (MRI) scanners per million population, with the exception of Poland and France.

The decline in the number of acute care beds per 1,000 population across Europe probably reflects an overall improvement in people's health and higher standards of primary care but, in contrast to the other European countries, the decline in the UK has been minimal, which has, probably appropriately, put the UK into the same territory as the other major European nations.

Table 1.2   Selected health data

	Acute care beds per 1,000 population		Practising physicians per 1,000 population		MRI scanner units per million population	
	2003	1993	2003	1993	2003	1993
Austria	6.0	6.7	3.4	2.5	13.5	5.9
France	3.8	4.9	3.4	3.2	2.8	1.4
Germany	6.6	7.7	3.4	2.9	6.0	1.4
Italy	3.9	5.8	4.1	3.8	11.6	2.5
Netherlands	3.2	4.1	3.1	2.6	n/a	2.5
Poland	5.1	5.8	2.5	2.2	1.0	n/a
Spain	3.1	3.5	3.2	2.5	7.3	2.1
Sweden	2.4	3.4	3.3	2.7	7.9	3.9
Switzerland	3.9	6.1	3.6	3.1	14.2	n/a
UK	3.7	3.9	2.2	1.7	5.2	n/a

Source: OECD (2005) *Health Data.*

Tables 1.1 and 1.2 highlight that spending on healthcare in the UK has improved dramatically since 1997, but we still lag behind spending in other European countries despite a concerted government effort since 1997 to improve the NHS through substantial increases in funding and more joined-up healthcare policies. In the 2002 Budget, the Chancellor announced increases in health expenditure up to 2007/8. In England, this was the largest-ever sustained increase in any five-year period in the history of the NHS.

There have been measurable benefits of the increased spending. In particular, waiting lists have fallen (see Figure 1.1).

The spending increase represents an annual average increase of 7.4 per cent in real terms between 2002/3 and 2007/8, and a total increase of 43 per cent in real terms over the period. Expenditure on the NHS has risen from £65 billion in 2002–3 to £87 billion in 2005, and is planned to reach £105 billion in 2007. And yet the task has only just begun. For all the extra investment, it is an equally natural reaction to call for more cash, but the torrent of additional funding is to be turned down, if not off, at the end of 2008.

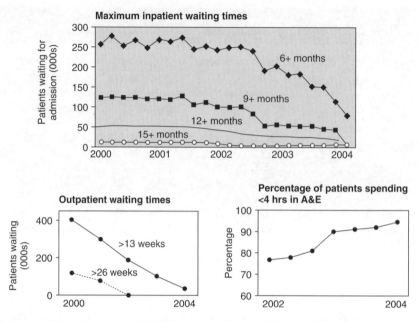

Source: Chief Executive's Report to the NHS, May 2004, http://www.dh.gov.uk/en/ Publicationsandstatistics/Publications/PublicationsPolicyAnd Guidance/DH_4081823.

Figure 1.1   Measurable benefits of increased spending on the NHS

In the coming years, even more outcomes have to be achieved in the NHS to balance costs against patient benefit; mass-market delivery against an individually tailored, needs-based service; clinical standards and efficacy against innovation and medical developments; regulatory control against informed choice; and effective management against devolved responsibility.

But much of the extra spending has been wasted . . .

The government has put a lot more money into the NHS, but poor management has, tragically, squandered much of it.

A lot of the new money went on increasing staffing, and paying people more. Given the impoverishment of the system prior to 1997, some have argued that this is a one-off correction in pay levels that was justified. This is the view expressed by Gill Morgan at the NHS Confederation:

In 2004/05 most of the new money (73 per cent) was spent on existing services that were chronically underfunded. This included 30 per cent on employing new staff and 20 per cent on increasing pay. Other costs included drugs, improving buildings and technology. Twenty per cent of the new money was spent on providing new services and seven per cent is expected to be released from efficiency improvements.[2]

But the King's Fund paints a different picture:[3]

Its [the King's Fund] analysis shows that much of it [the extra spending] has gone on 'hidden costs'. In the past year, around 29 per cent of the money set aside for hospitals and community services was spent on . . . NHS pensions, known as rebasing, which is the cost of transferring infla-tion-proofed pensions from the Treasury to the Department of Health.[4]

The next biggest chunk, 27 per cent, went on pay increases for staff. Another 12 per cent went on staffing reforms – the cost of modernising contracts with doctors and staff, which are aimed at getting them to work more flexibly in return for extra pay.

Setting aside money for medical negligence claims took up a further 5 per cent. After all this was allowed for, just 2.4 per cent was left over for providing new beds and extra operations – barely above the rate of inflation.

Most of the extra expenditure, in other words, has been eaten up by administration and staffing costs. We have not had value for money. Although there has been some improvement in 2005/6 and in the projected expenditure for 2006/7, the prospects still look bleak.

As the King's Fund put it:

As in previous years, next year a significant proportion of the extra cash for the NHS will go on higher pay. This is not in itself a bad thing – helping to retain and attract staff, for example. However, with consul-tant and nurse rates already near the top of the international league table, it raises questions about value for money.[5]

Furthermore

While the situation in 2006/7 looks better than in the current year, the Department of Health has decided to raise the tariff price for the work hospitals do by only 1.5 per cent – well below the inflation rate for NHS costs. This will potentially leave hospitals with less cash than we estimate to meet other development targets.[6]

Of the £4.5 billion cash increase in 2006/7 for hospital and community health services in England, 72 per cent will be absorbed by higher pay and other cost pressures.

Even if you could accept the argument that the National Health Service had some catching up to do in terms of pay and conditions, there is every expectation that when the money moves away from pay rises, it will not be spent wisely. Poor decision-making, poor negotiations (with the unions that have taken the extra spending), poor analysis (on trade-offs, for example) and poor implementation will mean that the British people will continue to get poor value for money – and this will continue until the organizational dynamics and poor management issues are addressed.

One small example, repeated, probably, in many other places, is the case of Ravenscourt Park Hospital. A decision was made to enter into a long-term lease (15 years) based on the belief that London lacked hospital capacity (which even a cursory piece of analysis would have shown to be wrong). It has been clear to the author for at least two years that the site needed to be closed down – not only was it losing, at that time, £12 million a year, but a 30-minute back-of-the-envelope economic calculation

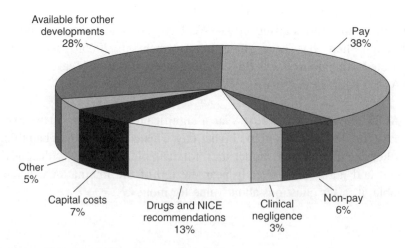

Source: King's Fund Briefing, 12 December 2005.

Figure 1.2   Spending on the NHS 2006/2007

suggested that its break-even point was as much as 140 per cent of capacity – in other words, it could never make money. This analysis was given to the decision-makers in 2004 – and, at the time of writing, after £24 million of taxpayers' money has been wasted, and a hefty bill paid to McKinsey, the management consultant company to come to the same conclusion, the decision has finally been made to close it:

Hospital hailed as future of the NHS is forced to close
The Times today reports that a hospital leased four years ago by the NHS is to be closed for lack of patients. Ravenscourt Park Hospital in West London – the former Royal Masonic Hospital – was acquired by Hammersmith Hospitals NHS Trust in 2002 on a 15-year lease. It was lauded by ministers at the time as being the future of elective surgery, a dedicated NHS centre concentrating on a limited number of procedures and offering top-class facilities. During the four years since it was leased, 18,500 operations have been conducted at the hospital, an average of about 4,500 a year. But this was uneconomic, and the hospital was losing £12 million a year. To break even it needed to treat 11,000 to 12,000 patients a year. (Summary from *The Times*, August 2006)

The pay rises that have taken up the bulk of the increased spending have been poorly managed. Such a massive increase in staffing and pay rates should produce greatly enhanced morale, motivation and productivity, but in the perverse NHS, exactly the opposite has happened. GPs – major beneficiaries of the increased spending – have reduced the hours they work and increased their take-home pay, yet their morale is at an all-time low. Patients are increasingly frustrated at the 9 to 5, 5-days-a-week working practices of GP surgeries. An increase in spending has resulted in unhappy GPs and a poorer service for patients. This is poor management. Similarly, the hospital consultants and nurses are better paid but probably more disaffected from the NHS, their employer, than at any time in the history of the service.

Dr Maurice Slevin, a consultant medical oncologist at Bart's and the London NHS Trust, in a book written for the Centre for Policy Studies, says bureaucracy and poor management are rife throughout the NHS. Dr Slevin highlights the high prevalence of managers in the NHS and claims that in private hospitals there are just under two managers for every 10 nurses, whereas in the NHS there are eight managers for every ten nurses:[7] 'In the NHS, the vast numbers of managers are there to stop things happening. In the private sector, the small numbers of managers are there to make things happen.'[8] Dr Slevin also points out that, in September 2001, there were 62,500 doctors, including 31,700 trainees, employed by the NHS in England, whereas in comparison there were 252,760 management and support staff (his source: www.doh.gov.uk/stats/doctors.htm). On balance it is now widely acknowledged by the government, many clinicians and others, that the NHS is over-centralized and predominately run as a top-down, one-size-fits-all bureaucracy.

There are a number of NHS hospitals around the country that are being managed poorly in terms of both their financial performance, and probably also in terms of their clinical performance. Evidence suggests that the spectrum from the worst-performing NHS hospitals to the best is large and growing. In 2004, 65 NHS Trusts (24 per cent) failed to achieve financial balance compared to 50 in 2003 (18 per cent). Of these, twelve NHS Trusts reported substantial deficits of over £5 million in 2004, compared to seven in 2003[9] (see Table 1.3). And this occurs at a time when spending

Table 1.3 NHS Trusts with deficits of over £5 million

NHS Trust	Deficit (£ million)	2003–4 Deficit before support (£ million)	NHS Trust	2002–3 Deficit (£ million)
Mid Yorkshire Hospitals	(18.6)	(30.6)	North Bristol	(44.6)
Worcestershire Acute Hospitals	(12.8)	(12.8)	Royal United Hospital Bath	(24.8)
			East Kent Hospitals	(11.4)
Maidstone and Tunbridge Wells	(9.0)	(9.0)	Worcestershire Acute Hospitals	(9.9)
Brighton and Sussex	(7.9)	(11.4)	United Bristol Healthcare	(9.3)
Plymouth Hospitals	(7.8)	(11.0)	South Manchester University Hospitals	(7.0)
Royal Wolverhampton Hospital	(7.6)	(7.6)	Royal Cornwall Hospitals	(5.2)
Royal Cornwall Hospitals	(5.8)	(15.3)		
Essex Rivers Healthcare	(5.8)	(5.8)		
Southampton University Hospitals	(5.4)	(8.4)		
Kings Lynn and Wisbech Hospitals	(5.4)	(5.4)		
Buckinghamshire Hospitals	(5.2)	(9.2)		
Good Hope Hospital	(5.0)	(5.0)		

Source: Financial Management in the NHS, joint report by the National Audit Office and the Audit Commission, June 2005.

on the NHS has nearly doubled over five years. It should be an urgent priority to find ways of closing this gap: in poorly-managed hospitals the local citizens are getting a poor service, and taxpayers' money is being wasted.

And the UK still compares poorly with other developed nations in terms of health outcomes

Of course, it will take time for any increased spending to work through to health outcomes, but the prospects are not good; the UK ranks poorly in terms of health outcomes.

A new guide on NHS treatment by the Dr Foster healthcare group has found that 5,000 lives could be saved by 'slightly improving' current hospital treatment. The same report also found that:

> There is significant variation between hospitals in both outcomes and standards of care. Mortality rates (2002–2005) vary from 22% above expected at Burton Hospitals NHS Trust to 27% below at Royal Free Hampstead NHS Trust . . . The NHS is not using its resources as efficiently as it could be. By reducing length of stays last year, hospitals in England could have saved £4.5 billion . . . Hospitals are not doing enough to find out what patients want from their services in order to meet their needs.[10]

It is clear that the UK is remaining resolutely at the bottom of the league table of poorly-performing healthcare economies. Once again, the government should be encouraged – it is trying to do the right things, and it has made improvements (especially on waiting lists), but until the core problems of the NHS are addressed – dysfunctional organization and poor management – then the extra money, the intelligent policy, the commitment and the drive of politicians and their advisers and, most importantly, the reasonable expectations of patients and taxpayers, will be thwarted.

This section finishes by looking at some of the data on international comparisons of health outcomes.

The core theme of this book is that the Labour government has got two things right out of the three that are wrong with the NHS: they have spent more money, and they are putting into place sensible policy. However, unless they address the third problem – dysfunctional organizational dynamics and poor management – then much of the extra money spent will be wasted, and reform will collapse.

It would, though, be churlish and inaccurate to claim that progress has not been made. The NHS had, by 1997 when Labour came to power, become dangerous. A report on quality in the NHS[11] cites the Wanless Report:

> Using 2001 OECD data, the Wanless Report shows that UK health expenditures were 6.8% of gross domestic product, compared with the European Union (EU) average of 7.9% and an income-weighted EU average of 8.4%. The Labour Government has committed to a multi-year infusion of significant new levels of health spending, as well as to an aggressive recruitment and retention strategy to increase the workforce. [Issues identified by the Wanless Commission in 1997 were]
>
> • Fewer doctors and nurses employed per head than in most European countries, at 1.7 doctors and 4.5 nurses per 1,000 population. These figures were from 1997, when the Labour Government began its reforms of the NHS, including the Quality Agenda.
> • Lags behind other countries in adopting and diffusing new technologies, in part explained by 'cash-limited budgets and greater central control over technology-adoption decisions'.
> • Less technology per capita. Number of CT (Computerised Tomography) and MRI (Magnetic Resonance Imaging) scanners below the EU average of 15 million of the population.
> • Uptake of new drugs is at most half of that in Germany, and a third of that in France.

We started, then, from a long way back – and both political parties have to take responsibility for this neglect through the 1970s and 1980s, and most of the 1990s. The Labour government has made positive progress. The reduction in waiting lists has been identified previously, but it is worth stressing the point here. In the Leatherman and Sutherland report, they quote DH data:[12] 'Number of patients waiting over 12 months for heart surgery: 1,093 in 2000; none in 2002. Number of patients waiting over 9 months for heart surgery: 2,694 in 2000, 212 in 2002. Consultant cardiologists: 467 in 1999; 590 in 2002.' Access has improved. In a related publication, Leatherman and Sutherland write '[Thrombolysis rates after Acute Myocardial Infarction] In March, 2002, 59% of patients were treated within 30 minutes of arriving at hospital. By September 2004, this figure had increased to 84%. The proportion of people being

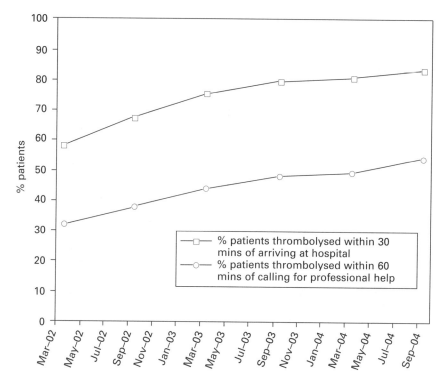

Source: Royal College of Physicians, 2005.

Figure 1.3 Thrombolysis rates post-acute myocardial infarction, England 2002–04

thrombolysed within one hour of calling for professional help, which is clinically more meaningful, was 32% in March 2002 and 54% in September 2004' (see Figure 1.3).[13]

Service in A&E (Accident and Emergency) has also improved – driven by high-profile government targeting: '82% of UK respondents indicated that they were treated in A&E in less than four hours, a figure broadly in line with comparator countries (Australia 87%, Canada, 74%, USA 87%)' (see Figure 1.4).[14]

The extra spending, to use a final example, has increased clinical staffing, and the number of clinicians has increased with the government's extra spending (but, again, from a very low start): 'The UK has a low level of practising physicians per 1000 population relative to comparator countries. The UK figures have increased in recent years' (see Figure 1.5).[15]

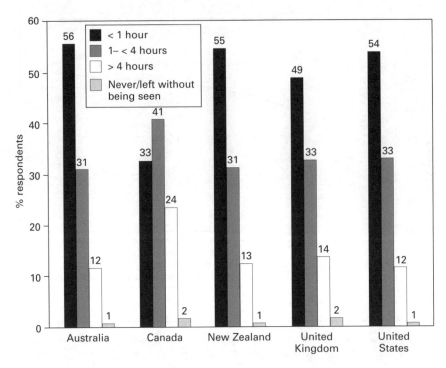

Source: Commonwealth Fund, 2004.

Figure 1.4   Waits in Accident and Emergency, international comparison 2004

So the Government has made progress, and, as has been said before, it is the only government (more accurately, Tony Blair is the only Minister) since Clement Atlee's (with Bevan as Minister of Health) that has taken on this thorny issue of healthcare reform – so these criticisms should be gilded with significant praise. But, neither should the government be over-credited with achievement – it is important to get this right.

Many of the improvements in clinical outcomes, which will be outlined shortly, are not a result of a better NHS, but because of two things:

1. *A combination of public health campaigns and lifestyle changes.* Reference will be made shortly to the (positive) impact on heart disease of the stop-smoking campaign. The government can take due credit for its persistence and resolve in this area.

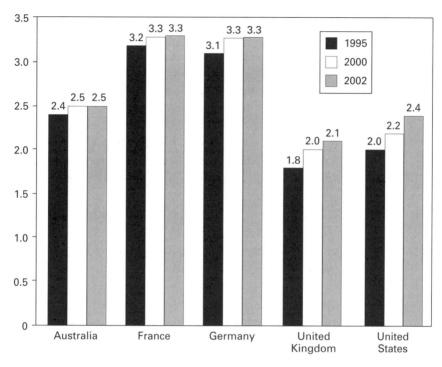

Source: OECD *Health Data*, 2004.

Figure 1.5   Practising physicians (head count) per 1000 population, international comparison, 1995, 2000, 2002

2.   *Medical practice.* Doctors are hugely committed to their patients – that is why they became doctors; they are alert to innovations that can improve patient outcomes and introduce them whenever they can. Medical science has advanced over the last few years – and this advance is an important driver of better medical outcomes. Unfortunately an increasing number of these innovations are made outside the UK (see Chapter 5). The distress of the NHS is not only damaging patient outcomes, it is also degrading our country's ability to build wealth.

There have been improvements in medical outcomes – and considering that the Labour government's commitment started only in 1997 – and probably more accurately in 2001, the progress has been commendable.

The bottom line is that UK health outcomes have improved significantly, but:

- A lot of this improvement has had little to do with the government – even the most uncontroversial of the three measures (money, as opposed to policy, and taking responsibility away from the Civil Service) has not had as big an influence (because of the organization and poor Civil Service management) but rather to lifestyle changes. But, to repeat, the government can take *some* credit for these changes.
- Waiting Lists have fallen, but the financial mismanagement of the system (and the consequent waste) will result in even this achievement being reversed. The news report listed below is typical of what we will hear increasingly over the next few months:

  Debt-ridden trusts halt IVF treatment
  Infertile couples in Northamptonshire are to be denied IVF treatment on the NHS by three primary care trusts facing a £38m deficit. The three trusts, which will merge into Northamptonshire PCT from next month, have suspended treatment for all couples. (*Guardian*, June 2004, p. 11)

- Clinical outcomes *have* been improving, but:
  o Our position relative to other advanced countries has not improved. The interpretation of this is, of course, complicated, but the conclusion that something – organization and management, in the view that this book takes – is confounding progress is unarguable.
  o Inequities – that is, the benefit levels between different social classes – have been increasing. In other words, the middle class is getting healthier and the poorer classes are becoming less healthy.

Both of these propositions are discussed below.

Death as a result of coronary disease has fallen. Leatherman and Sutherland,[16] quoting ONS (Office for National Statistics) figures, show that in 1995–7, 141.5 people died of circulatory disease per 100,000 population. In 1996–8, it was 135.7; in 1997–99, 128.7; in 1998–2000, 122.0; and in 1999–2001, 114.8. And it is likely that this trend is continuing. Leatherman and Sutherland say, 'UK mortality rates from circulatory disease have shown a marked decrease. UK rates were similar to the EU average rate in 1999 although they were among the highest of the comparator countries. In the UK, the drop in mortality rates was 55% for both males and females in the 30 years between 1972 and 2002' (see Figure 1.6).

But progress against our comparator countries is poor:[17] 'In 1999, the UK had the highest mortality rate in people aged below 75 years from coronary heart disease among the comparator countries. Compared to France, UK mortality rates were four times higher for females and around three times higher for males' (see Figure 1.7). These rates have, however, been falling, from about 250 deaths per 100,000 population in 1997 to about 200 in 2002[18] (see Figure 1.8). As mentioned above, a large part of this reduction is a result of fewer people smoking: 'Smoking cessation was the largest contributor to the declining mortality rate from coronary heart disease; it was estimated to account for almost half of the rate of decline. Clinical processes and treatment contributed 42% of the overall deaths prevented or postponed; personal risk factors or behavioural factors contributed 58% (see Figures 1.9 and 1.10).[19]

This pattern – of an improving picture, but a persistently poor performance compared to other advanced countries – is true also in breast cancer: 'Despite a 21% reduction between 1990 and 1999, England continued to have the highest breast cancer mortality rates among these comparator countries: 28.9 deaths per 100,000 compared to the lowest rate in Australia with 21.9 per 100,000[20] (see Figure 1.11). Of the 5 countries compared, the US had the highest survival rates from breast cancer, with 86% of women alive five years after diagnosis; and England had the lowest, with 75%' (see Figure 1.12).[21]

Not only is the UK not closing the gap with other advanced economies, but inequity within the UK is increasing. One of the defences the unions make for keeping the monopoly NHS in the public sector is that it is equitable. This is patently false. The free NHS, as was argued earlier, spends more on the middle class than it does on the lower classes. The results of this inequity are clear in the figures on clinical outcomes. Taking just one example, infant mortality rates by social class, deaths per 1,000 live births has reduced from 4.3 in 1997 for the professional,

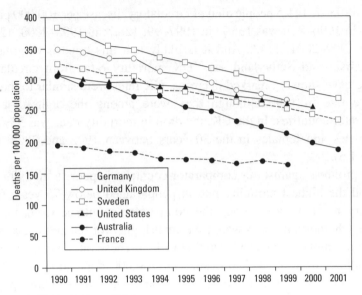

Source: OECD *Health Data*, 2004.

Figure 1.6(a) Mortality rates from circulatory disease, international comparison 1990–2001

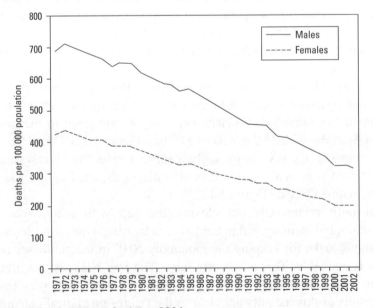

Source: Office for National Statistics, 2004.

Figure 1.6(b) Mortality rates from circulatory disease, UK 1971–2002

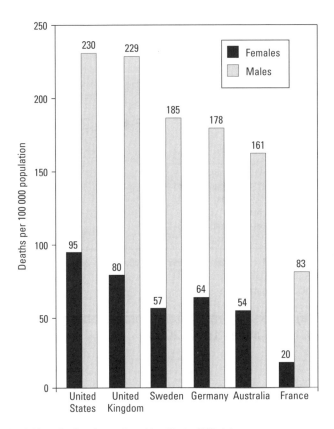

Source: WHO Mortality Database, from HeartStats ONS data.

Figure 1.7 Mortality rates from coronary heart disease (35–74 years), international comparison 1999–2000

managerial and technical classes to 3.8 in 2000. For unskilled manual it has risen from 7.9 in 1997 to 8.0 in 2000.[22]

Consistent with the major theme of this book, performance metrics more clearly associated with the quality of management, as opposed to behavioural changes in the population or advances in medical science, are at best static: 'The number of operations cancelled at the last minute for non-clinical reasons has made no significant sustained improvement over the past 6 years [to 2004].'[23] A key hospital management task is to keep a clean hospital: 'The proportion of *Staph aureus* blood culture isolates that are methicillin-resistant (MRSA) varies widely across Europe. The highest proportion of MRSA was in Greece (44.4%); the lowest was in the

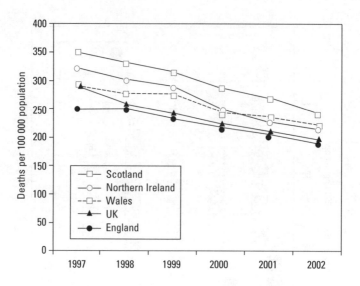

Source: HeartStats, ONS data.

Figure 1.8(a)   Mortality rates from coronary heart disease, males 35–74 years, UK countries 1997–2000

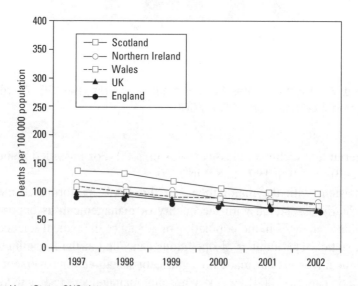

Source: HeartStats, ONS data.

Figure 1.8(b)   Mortality rates from coronary heart disease, females 35–74 years, UK countries 1997–2002

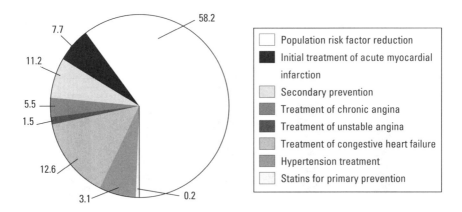

Source: Unal, B., Critchley, J.A. and Capewell, S. (2004) 'Explaining the decline in coronary heart disease mortality in England and Wales between 1981 and 2000', *Circulation*, 109(9): 1101–7.

Figure 1.9 Contributing factors in the decline in coronary heart disease mortality, England and Wales 1981–2000 (%)

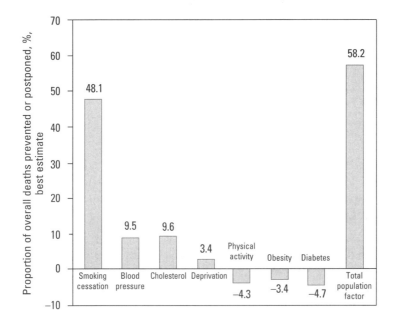

Source: as for Figure 1.9.

Figure 1.10 Proportion of death prevented or postponed as a result of population risk factor changes

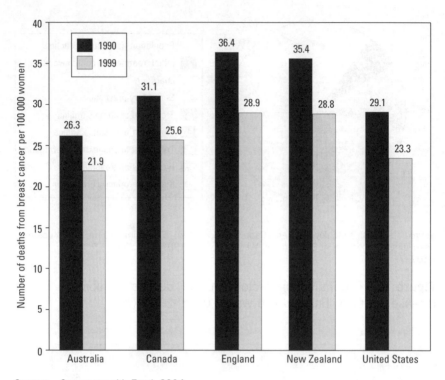

Source: Commonwealth Fund, 2004.

Figure 1.11   Mortality rates from breast cancer, international comparison 1990 and 1999

Netherlands (0.6%). The UK's result was among the highest at 41.5%'[24] (Figure 1.13). The unions have advanced a false and specious argument that it is where hospital cleaning has been outsourced to private companies that MRSA has increased. In the first place, as Confederation of British Industry (CBI) data shows, that is completely incorrect, and a deliberate distortion of the data. But it also typifies the warped thinking in the public sector. Whether a management team decides to do hospital cleaning in-house, or to outsource, management still retains the ultimate responsibility for results. If the outsourced contract is not being run well, then competent management would have the data to hand, and would either get immediate improvement from the sub-contractors or revoke the contract, bring the work in-house, or appoint another sub-contractor. But there are no circumstances in which a competent management team would

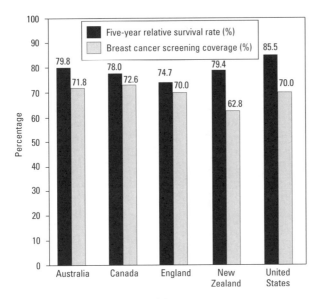

Source: Commonwealth Fund 2004.

Figure 1.12(a)   Breast cancer survival (~1992–97) and screening rates (~2000), international comparison

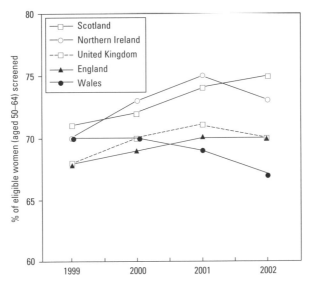

Source: Office for National Statistics.

Figure 1.12(b)   Breast screening coverage on women aged 50–64, UK countries 1992–2002

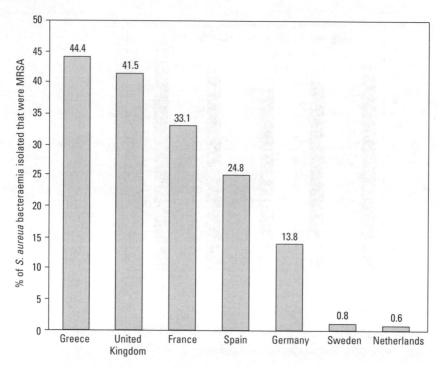

Source: Tiemersma E.W., Bronzwaer, S.L., Lyytikainen, O. *et al*. (2004) 'European Antimicrobial Resistance Surveillance System Participants Methicillin-resistant Staphylococcus aureus in Europe, 1999–2002', *Emerging Infectious Diseases*, 10(9): 1627–34.

Figure 1.13   MRSA bacteraemia as a proportion of all *Staphylococcus aureus* bacteraemias, international comparison, 1999–2002

absolve themselves of responsibility. It is significant that rates of MRSA in private hospitals in the UK are virtually non-existent, and far lower than even the rate in the Netherlands.

A final example of poor management is the fact that NHS managers/civil servants do not create an environment in which errors can be identified and corrected: 'Doctors in the UK rated the hospitals in which they work quite poorly in terms of their ability to find and address medical errors; only 3 per cent of respondents rated their hospital excellent' (Figure 1.14).[25]

Although there has been some return for the money spent (but not enough), it is becoming clear as the years of boom become tarnished by the waste created by poor management, that we are inevitably going to see the progress stall. Already waiting lists are beginning to lengthen again. The primary target over the last few years has been waiting lists, and all

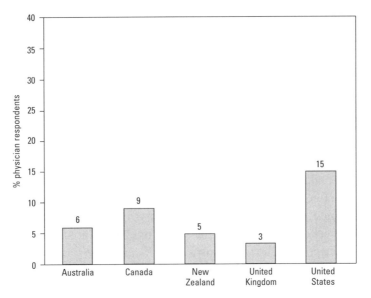

Source: Commonwealth Fund, 2000.

Figure 1.14(a) Hospitals rated excellent at finding and addressing medical error, international comparison, 2000

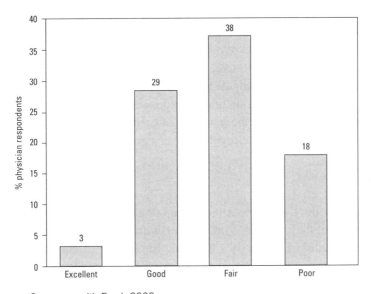

Source: Commonwealth Fund, 2000.

Figure 1.14(b) Physicians' ratings of hospital effectiveness in finding and addressing medical error, UK 2000

the attention has been focused on this issue. And they have fallen – to the huge benefit of patients. But the target has now shifted suddenly and completely to deficits. Waiting lists inevitably will rise. This monothematic management style, driven by the political or bureaucratic flavour of the day, is typical of what is wrong with the NHS, and why the organizational dynamics and quality of management have to change if things are to improve sustainably.

It has been argued so far in this book that a prerequisite to change is to gain good quality information and data – partly so that managers and clinicians can make better decisions, and partly because this is the information that patients and commissioners need in order to exercise informed choice, which in turn is one of the major drivers of creating a patient-responsive service. This part of the 'case for change' argument concludes with a description of how the mismanaged, chaotic system not only does not have the relevant information, but is also culturally biased against it. The evidence is taken from the Leatherman and Sutherland report that has been quoted extensively in this section.

Leatherman and Sutherland stress in their report how difficult it is to compile a report on quality in the NHS:

> Evaluating the quality of care in the NHS is challenging. Although a plethora of data exists, there is a shortage of easily accessible, validated datasets and analyses that portray quality in a fully credible and defensible manner. An authoritative, coherent and integrated set of analyses based on consensual standards with well-presented charts and graphs is needed to present a common understanding of quality in the NHS. In the absence of such, and for the purposes of compiling data for this project, we have attempted to pull together a very preliminary prototype.[26]

They go on to say:

> We present the data in both tables and charts, in part to illustrate the important issues in the content and format of dissemination and communication. To identify clearly the limitations of our research, we must explicitly admit to encountering numerous data and analytic problems. Enumeration of data issues not only provides appropriate caveats for data interpretation in this report, but also serves to describe the 'state of the art' of quality-related data in England. Below is an abbreviated list of four key data issues:

- Uncertainty regarding validity and reliability of data sources. There is little agreement on the types of extant data that are valid and for what purposes they are reliable. For example, Hospital Episode Statistics (HES), a large and important dataset, draws a range of opinions about its accuracy and completeness. Data collected, analysed and reported on in the DOH website will likewise incite a range of opinions as to its validity and reliability. There are adverse and very serious consequences of this contestability of data. Practically speaking, it allows for endless debate as to whether any analysis depicting quality performance is accurate. The controversy sometimes reflects a sincere concern for validity, at other times, it is a means of side-tracking the real issue of performance deficiencies.
- Standardised definitions for quality measures. Use of data for selected performance indicators is compromised because the definition of the measure changes over time. For instance, changes are made in the definition of the numerator and denominator populations for constructing a statistical measure.

   Performance indicators also change over time. For example, one indicator for effective cardiovascular care was administration of thrombolytic therapy within 30 minutes of arrival at the hospital. In 2003, the time interval was changed to 20 minutes. Further difficulties are encountered because some data series are for England only, others for England and Wales, and still others for the entire UK. These various datasets and the targets set against them are often poorly integrated and disparate.
- Use of longitudinal trending and time series. The Quality Agenda faces serious consequences because of unstable definitions in data and quantification of measures. A fundamental analytic tool for quality measurement and improvement is the identification of baseline performance and longitudinal trending across time to track progress or lack of progress. The rigour and credibility of time analyses or series analyses in England are undermined by the unstable data and quality measures.
- 'Compromises' in data entry and reporting. There are both intentional and unintentional distortions in data entry and collection. Honest errors or gaps in data entry and reporting occur for a number of reasons. One problem is that the frontline staff, upon whom data reporting depends, lack an understanding or credence

that the task is important enough to 'get right', which is compounded by their lack of training in the proper processes for accuracy.

The second type of 'compromise', sometimes called 'gaming', is intentional. It is an inherent vulnerability in any endeavour related to data submission, where positive or negative consequences are perceived. By widespread anecdote, and through some data validation performed in the DOH, we know that inaccuracies or distortions are present, particularly in areas such as waiting times (both inpatient and outpatient).[27]

The authors conclude:

The NHS has yet to harness the power of data. As well as a management tool, robust data can be a trigger for cultural change. By providing evidence of organisational and personal deficiencies, data can result in a felt need for change and motivation for action (Lewin, 1952).

Many in the NHS often view data with indifference or as a necessary evil offered up within a hierarchical and centrally commanded structure to be held to account, not as a useful tool to improve quality of care for patents within the local context. This may be rooted in concerns to protect professional autonomy, in perceptions about time and resource constraints, or in attitudes that data cannot capture complex situations. Alternatively, it may be the result of a negative spiral, whereby there is little regard for the value of data (other than as a means for satisfying central requirements) so little effort is expended on collecting timely and accurate data or meaningfully collating it. The resulting poor datasets are seen to provide an inaccurate picture of performance, thereby reinforcing the view that collecting data is not important.[28]

Recommendations from the Bristol enquiry have still not been implemented

Following clinical failures that resulted in the needless death of children, the Bristol Royal Infirmary was investigated in a process starting in 1998. The brief of the enquiry (http://www.bristol-inquiry.org.uk/index.htm) was:

To inquire into the management of the care of children receiving complex cardiac surgical services at the Bristol Royal Infirmary between 1984 and 1995 and relevant related issues; to make findings as to the adequacy of the services provided; to establish what action was taken both within and outside the hospital to deal with concerns raised about the surgery and to identify any failure to take appropriate action promptly; to reach conclusions from these events and to make recommendations which could help to secure high-quality care across the NHS.

It is worth quoting this thorough report in some detail. The failings of Bristol Royal Infirmary do not occur everywhere – and often where elements occur, things are not as dire as they were in Bristol. But the underlying diagnosis of the Bristol situation does apply to large parts of the NHS. In writing this book I obviously have not had the access and resources that the Bristol enquiry team had available to them. The veracity of the analysis and conclusions of this enquiry are unarguable. There is little evidence that there has been a systematic programme to make sure that the Bristol situation cannot occur elsewhere in the NHS. And the lack of quality data, outlined above, means that a similar situation would be difficult to spot.

On 3 September 2006, an eminent group of doctors declared their concerns that the recommendations have not been implemented, and that further disasters could well occur:

Arrogant surgeons 'risk another Bristol babies scandal'
Five years on, patients are dying on operating tables because some doctors are still failing to act on the lessons of the 'Bristol Babies' scandal that led to the deaths of 30 babies, according to the Royal College of Surgeons. The *Sunday Times* last weekend reported that more than 300 babies a year were being left with brain damage because of oxygen starvation caused by lack of proper care at birth. (*Sunday Times*, 3 September 2006, p. 7)

The following extracts from the Bristol report (http://www.bristol-inquiry.org.uk/index.htm) should be read with this worrying view in mind. The report continues its introduction by saying:

It is an account of healthcare professionals working in Bristol who were victims of a combination of circumstances which owed as much to general failings in the NHS at the time than any individual failing. Despite their manifest good intentions and long hours of dedicated work, there were failures on occasion in the care provided to very sick children.

It is an account of a service offering paediatric open-heart surgery which was split between two sites, and had no dedicated paediatric intensive care beds, no full-time paediatric cardiac surgeon and too few paediatrically trained nurses.

It is an account of a time when there was no agreed means of assessing the quality of care. There were no standards for evaluating performance. There was confusion throughout the NHS as to who was responsible for monitoring the quality of care.

It is an account of a hospital where there was a 'club culture'; an imbalance of power, with too much control in the hands of a few individuals.

It is an account in which vulnerable children were not a priority, either in Bristol or throughout the NHS.

And it is an account of a system of hospital care which was poorly organised. It was beset with uncertainty as to how to get things done, such that when concerns were raised, it took years for them to be taken seriously.

The circumstances of Bristol, and the NHS, at the time, led to the system for providing paediatric cardiac surgery (PCS) being flawed. All of these flaws, taken together, led to around one-third of all the children who underwent open-heart surgery receiving less than adequate care. More children died than might have been expected in a typical PCS unit. In the period from 1991 to 1995 between 30 and 35 more children under 1 died after open-heart surgery in the Bristol Unit than might be expected had the Unit been typical of other PCS units in England at the time.

Our Report contains close to 200 Recommendations. They include the following:

Children: the needs of very sick children in the 1980s and 1990s were not given a high priority. For the future, children in hospital must be cared for in a child-centred environment, by staff trained in caring for children and in facilities appropriate to their needs. A national director for children's healthcare services should be appointed to lead the development of child-centred healthcare.

Safety: the arrangements for caring for very sick children in Bristol at that time were not safe. There was too little recognition that the state of buildings and of equipment, and the training of the staff, could cause actual harm to the children. For the future, the NHS must root out unsafe practices. It must remove barriers to safe care. In particular, it must promote openness and the preparedness to acknowledge errors and to learn lessons. Healthcare professionals should have a duty of candour to patients. Clinical negligence litigation, as a barrier to openness, should be abolished. Safe care should be promoted and led by a non-executive member of every trust board.

The competence of healthcare professionals: there was no requirement on hospital consultants at that time (nor is there now) to keep their skills and knowledge up to date. Surgeons were able to introduce new techniques without any formal system of notification. For the future, it must be part of all healthcare professionals' contracts with a trust (and part of a GP's terms of service) that they undergo appraisal, continuing professional development and revalidation to ensure that all healthcare professionals remain competent to do their job.

Organisation: consultants enjoyed (and still enjoy) what is virtually a job for life. Their relationship with the trust that employs them makes it difficult to bring about change. All employees should be treated in a broadly similar manner. Doctors, nurses and managers must work together as healthcare professionals, with comparable terms of employment and clear lines of accountability, in order to provide the best possible care for patients.

Standards of care: parents taking their children to be treated in Bristol assumed that the level of care provided would be good. Their children were cared for in a 'supra regional centre' designated as such by the Department of Health. They trusted the system. Few had any idea that there were no agreed standards of care for PCS or for any other specialty. For the future, there must be two developments. There must be agreed and published standards of clinical care for healthcare professionals to follow, so that patients and the public know what to expect. There must also be standards for hospitals as a whole. Hospitals which do not meet these standards should not be able to offer services within the NHS.

Openness: Bristol was awash with data. There was enough information from the late 1980s onwards to cause questions about mortality rates to be raised both in Bristol and elsewhere had the mindset to do so existed. Little, if any, of this information was available to the parents or to the public. Such information as was given to parents was often

partial, confusing and unclear. For the future, there must be openness
about clinical performance. Patients should be able to gain access to
information about the relative performance of a hospital, or a particular service or consultant unit.

Monitoring: the clinicians in Bristol had no one to satisfy but themselves that the service which they provided was of appropriate quality.
There was no systematic mechanism for monitoring the clinical performance of healthcare professionals or of hospitals. For the future there
must be effective systems within hospitals to ensure that clinical
performance is monitored. There must also be a system of independent
external surveillance to review patterns of performance over time and
to identify good and failing performance.

The aim of these and all our recommendations is to produce an NHS
in which patients' needs are at the centre and in which systems are in
place to ensure safe care and to maintain and improve the quality of
care.

We concentrate on open-heart surgery on children under 1. We adopt
a 'systems' approach to analysis, by which poor performance and errors
are seen as the product of systems which are not working well, as much
as the result of any particular individual's conduct. We acknowledge at
the outset that in a number of ways the service was adequate or more
than adequate. The great majority of children who underwent PCS in
Bristol are alive today.

Our overall conclusion, however, is that the PCS service for children
who received open-heart surgery was, on a number of criteria, less than
adequate.

To the extent that it is based on reliable and verifiable evidence, this
is the judgment of hindsight. At the time, while the PCS service was
less than adequate, it would have taken a different mindset from the one
that prevailed on the part of the clinicians at the centre of the service,
and senior management, to come to this view. It would have required
abandoning the principles which then prevailed: of optimism, of 'learning curves', and of gradual improvements over time. It would have
required them to adopt a more cautious approach rather than 'muddling
through'. That this did not occur to them is one of the tragedies of
Bristol.

We reach one conclusion which owes nothing to hindsight. There
was poor teamwork and this had implications for performance and
outcome. The crucial importance of effective teamwork in this complex

area of surgery was very widely recognised. Effective teamwork did not always exist at the Bristol Royal Infirmary. There were logistical reasons for this: for example the cardiologists could not be everywhere. The point is that everyone just carried on. In addition, relations between the various professional groups were on occasions poor. All the professionals involved in the PCS service were responsible for this shortcoming. But, in particular, this poor teamwork demonstrates a clear lack of effective clinical leadership. Those in positions of clinical leadership must bear the responsibility for this failure and the undoubtedly adverse effect it had on the adequacy of the PCS service.

The Experts to the Inquiry advised that Bristol had a significantly higher mortality rate for open-heart surgery on children under 1 than that of other centres in England. Between 1988 and 1994 the mortality rate at Bristol was roughly double that elsewhere in five out of seven years. This mortality rate failed to follow the overall downward trend over time which can be seen in other centres. Our Experts' statistical analysis also enabled them to find that a substantial and statistically significant number of excess deaths, between 30 and 35, occurred in children under 1 undergoing PCS in Bristol between 1991 and 1995. As our Experts make clear, 'excess deaths' is a statistical term which refers to the number of deaths observed over and above the number which would be expected if the Unit had been 'typical' of other PCS units in England. The term does not refer to any particular child's death. The mortality rate over the period 1991–1995 was probably double the rate in England at the time for children under 1, and even higher for children under 30 days. This higher mortality rate in Bristol was not restricted to the neonatal Switch and Atrio-Ventricular Septal Defect (AVSD) operations. Even without taking these two higher-risk groups into account, there was considerable evidence of divergent performance in Bristol. Further, differences in mortality rates in Bristol could not be accounted for on the ground of case mix (an explanation which some clinicians both then and even now have adopted).

Particular elements of the PCS service which were less than adequate

The system and culture of management in Bristol

Bristol was not unusual in having problems. It was, after all, managing the transition from the known (the old NHS) to the unknown (Trust status). Problems arise in all institutions. But it is incumbent on senior management to devise systems which respond quickly and effectively to these problems. What was unusual about Bristol was that the systems and culture in place were such as to make open discussion and review more difficult. Staff were not encouraged to share their problems or to speak openly. Those who tried to raise concerns found it hard to have their voice heard.

We accept that Dr Roylance, the Chief Executive of the Trust, was both thoughtful and principled in his development of a management system for what was one of the newest and largest trusts in England. He also succeeded in meeting the principal obligation of balancing the books. Sadly, a system of separate and virtually independent clinical directorates, combined with a message that problems were not to be brought to the Chief Executive for discussion and resolution, meant that there was power but no leadership. The environment was one in which problems were neither adequately identified nor addressed.

Nor were there effective measures outside Bristol to monitor the approach adopted by Dr Roylance. This was a feature of the NHS reforms in 1989–1991. Senior managers were invited to take control, but little or no system existed to monitor what they did in the exercise of that control. Indeed, it did not really exist inside the Trust either. The Chairman and the Trust Board were either part of the 'club' or treated as outsiders. Referring to information about the outcome of care, Mr McKinlay, the Chairman of the United Bristol Hospital Trust (UBHT) from 1994 onwards, told us that:

> there was no tradition or culture in UBHT that the Board or the committees of the Board should be involved . . . I thought that was something that was wrong. I thought the Board should have some knowledge of statistical outcome, but there was a tightrope to be trod to find a way of easing it into place.

Monitoring the quality of care
At a national level there was confusion as to who was responsible for monitoring quality of care. The confusion was not, however, just some administrative game of 'pass the parcel'. What was at stake was the health, welfare, and indeed the lives of children. What was lacking was any real system whereby any organization took responsibility for what a lay person would describe as 'keeping an eye on things'. The Supra Regional Services Advisory Group (SRSAG) thought that the health

authorities or the Royal College of Surgeons was doing it; the Royal College of Surgeons thought the SRSAG or the Trust was doing it, and so it went on. No one was doing it. We cannot say that the external system for assuring and monitoring the quality of care was inadequate. There was, in truth, no such system.

At a local level, although information arising from reviews of PCS emerged only rarely in the formal structures for audit within the Trust, or in the Trust's dealings with the District Health Authority, a good deal of activity did, in fact, take place. Moreover, it pre-dated the introduction of the formal system of medical audit in 1990. The clinicians involved in providing the PCS service collected, recorded and analysed data on procedures and deaths, set up and maintained computerised information systems, produced and circulated figures and reports, made annual returns to the national UK Cardiac Surgical Register (UKCSR) and received back aggregated data about national performance. They also held regular meetings to discuss the results of audit, and reviewed individual cases and series of cases.

The views of parents
The evidence of parents was mixed. To some, the staff, doctors, nurses and others were dedicated and caring and could not have done more. To others, some staff were helpful while others were not. To others again, the staff, largely the doctors and particularly the surgeons, were uncaring and they misled parents.

While the evidence is polarised, there is a strong sense that on many occasions communication between parents and some staff was poor. There does not appear to have been any deep thinking about how to communicate information to parents in advance of surgery, nor any systematised approach to doing so. While some parents felt that they had been significantly helped to understand what the surgery and subsequent intensive care involved, we were also told of doctors and nurses drawing diagrams on scraps of paper, or even a paper towel. The sense is gained that informing parents and gaining their consent to treatment was regarded as something of a chore by the surgeons.

As regards the process of gaining consent to surgery, it is difficult to imagine a more stressful time for parents whose children were about to undergo surgery. Their child was facing a major operation with an uncertain outcome and, to add to their great anxiety, they had the burden of responsibility of saying 'yes' or 'no' to that operation. That being so, the sharing of information should be a process. There must be time to take in what has been said by the clinicians, to reflect on it and to raise questions. This does not seem to have been the practice at Bristol, but neither would it have been regarded as poor practice elsewhere during the relevant period. With the benefit of hindsight it is clear that much distress and unhappiness will result if parents are not sympathetically allowed to find out what they wish to know about what is facing their child. It should not be a question of the healthcare professional judging what the parent needs to know: it is the parent who should make that decision. At the time, however, the prevailing view was that parents should be protected from too much information.

Conclusions on the adequacy of the service

The system for delivering PCS services in Bristol was frankly not up to the task. What we observed amounts to a failure of PCS services to thrive. There is real room for doubt as to whether open-heart surgery on the under-1s should have been designated a supra regional service in Bristol. With the benefit of hindsight, designation has all the qualities of a Greek tragedy: we know the outcome and yet are unable, from our point in time, to prevent it unfolding. Once designated, however, it simply never developed sufficiently well. We observe a paediatric open-heart service with high aspirations (including at one stage the ambition to become a centre for heart transplantation) simply overreaching itself, given its limitations, and failing to keep up with the rapid developments elsewhere in PCS during the late 1980s and early 1990s. In summary, opportunities were not taken. Exhaustion and low morale led to stagnation and an inability to move forward in response to new developments, despite the stimulus provided by a new generation of consultants.

Throughout the Inquiry we heard evidence of underfunding in Bristol, meaning that a gap had developed between the level of resources needed properly to meet the stated goals of the PCS unit and the level actually available. There were constant shortages in the supply of trained nursing staff, both for the operating theatre and the ICU. The complement of cardiologists and surgeons was always below the level deemed appropriate by the relevant professional bodies. The consultant cardiologists lacked junior support. They were expected to care for children in the Children's Hospital, and in the BRI operating theatre and ICU several hundred yards away down a steep hill, and to hold outreach clinics all over the South West and South Wales. The care of children undergoing PCS was split between two separate sites. Facilities for parents, and necessary medical equipment for children, had to be funded through the good offices of a charity, The Heart Circle.

It is crucial, however, to make clear the following. The inadequacy in resources for PCS at Bristol was typical of the NHS as a whole. From this, it follows that whatever went wrong at Bristol was not caused by lack of resources. Other centres laboured under the same or similar difficulties. For example, the shortage in qualified nurses and in cardiologists was a national phenomenon, affecting all centres. We therefore emphasise the point again that, while underfunding blighted the NHS as a whole, it does not alone provide the explanation for what went wrong in Bristol.

We note that in 2000, at last, the present Government acknowledged the gap between claim and reality in the NHS. A significant boost in funding was announced. A further commitment was made to align spending on the NHS with the average amount spent on healthcare in Europe. This development has been widely welcomed and is seen as a long-overdue recognition of the need for more resources. But, we add a caution. We have every reason to believe that to achieve what was set out in 'The NHS Plan' and is contemplated by our Report, there must be a sustained increase in funding year-on-year.

. . . We stress again that, to a very great extent, the flaws and failures of Bristol were within the hospital, its organisation and culture, and within the wider NHS as it was at the time . . .

The future:

We are required to 'make recommendations to secure high quality care across the NHS'.

We must learn the lessons of Bristol. Even today it is still not possible to say, categorically, that events similar to those which happened in Bristol could not happen again in the UK; indeed, are not happening at this moment.

That said we must not lose a sense of proportion. Every day the NHS provides a service to hundreds of thousands of patients, with which patients are satisfied and of which healthcare professionals can justifiably be proud.

In making our recommendations our guiding principles were:

- The complexity of the NHS as an organization must be recognised.
- Patients must be at the centre of the NHS, and thus the patient's perspective must be included in the policies, planning and delivery of services at every level.
- The dedication and commitment of NHS staff is and must remain at the core of the service.
- The quality of healthcare must include all aspects of care: clinical and non-clinical.
- Patients' safety must be the foundation of quality.
- Systems of care, and facilities, as well as individuals, affect the quality of healthcare.
- Learning from error, rather than seeking someone to blame, must be the priority in order to improve safety and quality.
- Openness and transparency are as crucial to the development of trust between healthcare professional and patient, as they are to the trust between the NHS and the public.
- The particular needs of children's healthcare services must be addressed.

The culture of the NHS

The culture of the future must be a culture of safety and of quality; a culture of openness and of accountability; a culture of public service; a culture in which collaborative teamwork is prized; and a culture of flexibility in which innovation can flourish in response to patients' needs.

Respect and honesty

Patients in their journey through the healthcare system are entitled to be treated with respect and honesty and to be involved, wherever possible, in decisions about their care.

The quality of healthcare would be enhanced by a greater degree of respect and honesty in the relationship between healthcare professional and patient. Good communication is essential, but as the Royal College of Surgeons of England told us: 'it is the area of greatest compromise in the practices of most surgeons in the NHS and the source of most complaints'.

Future doctors, nurses and other healthcare professionals must be adequately trained in communication skills during their initial education.

Partnership between patient and healthcare professional is the way forward. The exchange and provision of information is at the core of an open and honest relationship between healthcare professionals and patients. There are four fundamental principles which should in future underpin any policy aimed at meeting patients' needs for information. First, trust can only be sustained by openness. Secondly, openness means that information be given freely, honestly and regularly. Thirdly, it is of fundamental importance to be honest about the twin concerns of risk and uncertainty. Lastly, informing patients, and in the case of young children their parents, must be regarded as a process and not a one-off event.

Hospitals must have an integrated system of support and counselling for patients and carers, staffed by well-trained professionals with links to systems outside. Such a system is central to care, not an add on.

There should be a clear system in the form of a 'one-stop shop' in every trust for addressing the concerns of patients about the care provided or the conduct of a healthcare professional. When things go wrong hospitals and healthcare professionals have a duty of candour: to be open and honest. Not only does this show respect to patients; an error, once acknowledged, also allows lessons to be learned.

A Health Service which is well led
Patients are entitled to expect that both the NHS and the hospital in which they are cared for is well led. The highest priority still needs to be given to improving the leadership and management of the NHS at every level.

The role of government as regards the NHS in relation to the quality of care is twofold: to manage the NHS, and to organize good, comprehensive and independent systems to regulate the quality of healthcare.

Chief executives of trusts, particularly now that they are legally responsible for monitoring and improving the quality of healthcare, must be supported and enabled to carry out this duty. In particular, all employees, including consultants, must have a similar employment relationship with the trust.

Trust boards must be able to lead healthcare at the local level. Executive directors should be selected on agreed criteria and appropriately trained. Non-executives should play an active role in the affairs of the trust.

The quality of healthcare should be regulated through bodies such as the National Institute for Clinical Excellence and the Commission for Health Improvement. These bodies should be independent of government. There should be an independent overarching body, the Council for the Quality of Healthcare, to co-ordinate and integrate the activities of these bodies. This Council would report both to the Department of Health and to Parliament.

Competent healthcare professionals
A patient is entitled to be cared for by healthcare professionals with relevant and up-to-date skills and expertise.

The education of healthcare professionals in communication skills, the principles and organisation of the NHS, the development of teamwork, shared learning across professional boundaries, clinical audit, and leadership should be given greater priority.

Medical schools, schools of nursing and management schools should be encouraged to develop joint courses. Future healthcare professionals must work in multidisciplinary teams; shared learning should therefore begin as soon as possible. A common curriculum for the first year of undergraduate education of all healthcare professionals should be developed through a pilot project.

A system of regulation should be in place to ensure that healthcare professionals acquire and maintain professional competence. Regulation includes education, registration, training, continuing professional development, revalidation and discipline.

Medical schools must ensure that the criteria for selecting future doctors include the potential to be versatile, flexible and sensitive. They must also ensure that healthcare professionals are not drawn from too narrow an academic and socio-economic base.

Continuing Professional Development (CPD), periodic appraisal and revalidation must be compulsory for all healthcare professionals. There should be an overarching mechanism to co-ordinate and align the activities of the various bodies (the General Medical Council (GMC), the Nursing and Midwifery Council (NMC) and others) to ensure that they serve patients' interests. This mechanism should be a new independent Council for the Regulation of Healthcare Professionals (in effect, the body currently proposed in 'The NHS Plan'). This Council too should report to the Department of Health and to Parliament.

Senior managers in the NHS should be subject to CPD, periodic appraisal and revalidation.

There should be positive incentives to encourage senior clinicians to take on senior managerial roles, including special categories of registration with professional bodies and the ability to move out of and back into clinical practice after suitable retraining. There should be appropriate training for senior clinicians before taking on these roles.

Where surgeons or other clinicians undertake an invasive clinical procedure for the first time, they should be properly trained and directly supervised, if the procedure is already established. In the case of a new, untried invasive clinical procedure they must seek permission from the local research ethics committee for permission. Patients are entitled to know what experience the surgeon or clinician has before giving consent.

It must be the employer first and foremost who should be able to deal with poor performance and misconduct. Professional Codes of Conduct should be incorporated into healthcare professionals' contracts. It is for the relevant professional regulatory body to decide whether the healthcare professional's registration should be affected. For doctors, this body should be the GMC, for nurses the NMC.

The safety of care
Patients are entitled to care that is safe.

Around 5% of the 8.5 million patients admitted to hospitals in England and Wales each year experience an adverse event which may be preventable with the exercise of ordinary standards of care. How many of these events lead to death is not known but it may be as high as 25,000 people a year.

The components of safe care are much more than the actions or competence of healthcare professionals: they include the physical environment, equipment, working arrangements, teamwork and good communication.

The NHS is still failing to learn from the things that go wrong and has no system to put this right. This must change.

A culture of safety in which safety is everyone's concern must be created. Safety requires constant vigilance. Given that errors happen, they must be analysed with a view to anticipate and avoid them.

A culture of safety crucially requires the creation of an open, free, non-punitive environment in which healthcare professionals can feel safe to report adverse events and near misses (sentinel events).

The Government's proposed National Patient Safety Agency should be an independent agency to which certain sentinel events are reported so as to be analysed with a view to disseminating lessons throughout the NHS.

The culture of blame is a major barrier to the openness required if sentinel events are to be reported, lessons learned and safety improved. The system of clinical negligence is part of this culture of blame. It should be abolished. It should be replaced by effective systems for identifying, analysing, learning from and preventing errors and other sentinel events. An expert group should consider alternatives to clinical negligence, including an alternative administrative system of compensating those who suffer harm arising from medical care.

Incentives for reporting sentinel events should be introduced, whereby healthcare professionals' contracts would provide that they would be immune from disciplinary action from their employer or professional regulatory body if they were to report a sentinel event within 48 hours. Confidential reporting should be provided for. Failure to report would attract possible disciplinary action.

An approach to safety based on designing safer systems and equipment should be encouraged. The National Patient Safety Agency should bring together interested parties to tackle some of the more persistent causes of unsafe practices.

At trust board level, an executive director should be responsible for putting into operation the trust's strategy and policy on safety and a non-executive director should provide leadership to promote a culture of safety.

Care of an appropriate standard

Patients are entitled to care and treatment of an appropriate standard informed by current knowledge.

Until well into the 1990s, the notion that there should be explicit standards of care which all healthcare professionals should seek to meet and which would apply to patients across the NHS, simply did not exist. It is now widely accepted that this state of affairs has to change.

Patients are entitled to expect that their care will be of such quality as is consonant with good practice, based on sound evidence. Recent developments give cause for optimism. These include statutory responsibility of trusts for the quality of healthcare, the development of clinical guidelines through the National Institute for Clinical Excellence, and the monitoring of performance through the Commission for Health and Improvement.

There remains insufficient co-ordination in setting standards. Guidelines appear from a variety of bodies giving rise to confusion and uncertainty. Moreover, there are weaknesses in monitoring performance in relation to these standards, whether at the level of the trust or nationally. In particular there is no mechanism for surveillance to ensure that patterns of poor performance are recognised and addressed.

For the future, standards for clinical care must be set by the National Institute for Clinical Excellence. In doing so, it must draw on the expertise particularly of the Royal Colleges. Standards must be patient-centred. They must not be the product of individual professional groups talking to themselves. They must incorporate the concept of teamwork and the respective responsibilities of members of the team. Some standards should be obligatory, some to be achieved over time.

Generic standards for healthcare institutions
All hospitals must meet certain standards (generic standards). Those which do not should not be permitted to provide NHS services. Generic standards relate to such matters as the state of the buildings and of equipment, the quality of leadership and the trust's policies and procedures for ensuring that care is safe and of good quality.

Trusts must periodically undergo a process of validation and revalidation (akin to licensing), to ensure that they meet these standards. Revalidation would mean that the trust could continue to offer healthcare services. The Commission for Health Improvement would be responsible for the process of validation. In time the process of validation should be extended to discrete, identifiable services within a trust. A pilot project involving children's acute hospital services and paediatric cardiac surgery in particular should be carried out.

Information about performance in the NHS is the basic building block of any system of standards and quality. In the past, there have been great difficulties in collecting information.

There has also been a separation between administrative and clinical systems which our Experts described as 'wasteful and anachronistic'.

For the future the multiple methods and systems for collecting data must be reduced. Data must be collected as the by-product of clinical care.

At a national level, the monitoring of clinical performance should be brought together and co-ordinated by one body, an independent Office for Monitoring Healthcare Performance which would be part of the Commission for Health Improvement. It could also carry out a surveillance role.

Public involvement through empowerment
The public are entitled to expect that means exist for them to become involved in the planning, organisation and delivery of healthcare.

A patient-centred service is one that is designed and planned to address the needs of the particular sectors of the public it exists to serve. Strategic planning at national level, and decisions at local level must involve the public.

In its everyday working the NHS must take account of and respond to the interests and needs of the public.

The public must be involved in those processes designed to secure the competence of healthcare professionals, particularly in those bodies charged with setting standards for education, training and Continuing Professional Development.

The principles which should inform future policy about involving the public and patients in the NHS include:

• Patients and the public are entitled to be involved wherever decisions are taken about care in the NHS.
• The involvement of patients and the public must be embedded in the structures of the NHS and permeate all aspects of healthcare.
• The public and patients should have access to relevant information.
• Healthcare professionals must be partners in the process of involving the public.
• There must be honesty about the scope of the public's involvement, since some decisions cannot be made by the public.
• There must be transparency and openness in the procedures for involving the public and patients.
• The mechanisms for involvement should be evaluated for their effectiveness.
• The public and patients should have access to training and funding to allow them fully to participate.
• The public should be represented by a wide range of individuals and groups and not by particular 'patients' groups'.

> • The priority for involving the public should be that their interests are embedded into all organisations and institutions concerned with quality of performance in the NHS: in other words, the public should be 'on the inside', rather than represented by some organisation 'on the outside'.

Only by addressing the concerns raised in this book, and introducing its recommendations, will the 'culture' of the NHS be changed sufficiently to ensure that the situation that occurred in Bristol will really become just a horrible memory rather than a nightmare waiting to reappear at any minute. The Bristol Enquiry accords with the analysis in this book. At its core, this is an organizational and managerial failure. The inward-looking, insular NHS management and the managerially-incompetent politicians and civil servants are not the people who should be managing the service – safeguarding voters' and citizens' interest, yes – but not managing the service.

Customer/patient views

This chapter has so far tried to build a rationale for change. But really, the only important rationale for change is the answer to the question 'Are the customers (patients and taxpayers) content or do they want change?' This question is asked so infrequently, and is evidence of just how much the NHS has become a public sector playground rather then a serious citizen-centred service. The public is unhappy and it wants change. No further argument is necessary to face down the unions.

The experience of patients in the private sector ISTCs has been excellent – better, despite all the unsubstantiated horror stories generated by the unions, than in the NHS. And no NHS patient who went to a well-run, efficient and clinically effective private-sector hospital said 'That was great, but next time I want to get inferior treatment, in an MRSA-rampant hospital because I believe in civil servants.' The following set of diagrams illustrates the public mood. Countervailing claims are made that British citizens complain generally about the NHS, but like their local service. Their local service is delivered by doctors and nurses who really care, and who are battling against a dysfunctional organization and chronically poor management. Their commitment, skill and dedication are the concerned, smiling and reassuring faces that many patients see on the frontline, and

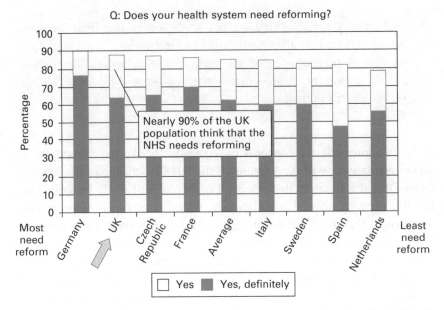

Q: Does your health system need reforming?

Source: Impatient for Change: European Attitudes to Healthcare Reform, Stockholm Network and Populus, 2004.

Figure 1.15   Citizen perceptions of healthcare quality

which cause them to praise their local service. They are absolutely right to do so – and it is unfortunate that the opponents of reform use this caring bond to justify the status quo.

Figure 1.15 shows that nearly 90 per cent of the British public believe that the NHS needs to be reformed. Reading the newspaper headlines, there is a strong impression that the government is swimming against the tide in its attempts to reform the system, but Figure 1.16 shows there is huge popular support for their efforts. In answer to a slightly different question Figure 1.16 shows that nearly 75 per cent of the population believe reform is necessary.

Figure 1.17 shows that the citizenry is aware that our lead in healthcare has eroded badly over the last thirty years. Only 10 per cent of the UK population believe that the NHS is the best system in Europe.

Much of what has been written about in this first chapter – the poor quality of data, the dysfunctional organizational dynamics and the chronically poor management – are, for the most part, hidden from the public. The need to wait for treatment is, of course, not hidden. Once again, the

Question: The NHS was the right idea when it was introduced in the 1940s, but Britain has changed so do we need a different healthcare system now?

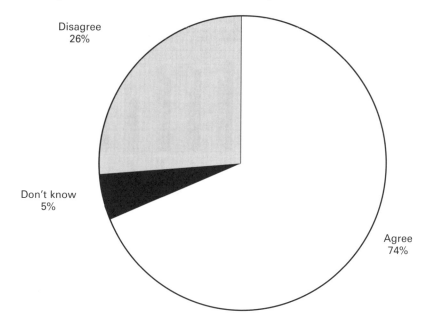

Disagree
26%

Don't know
5%

Agree
74%

Source: NHS Survey, February 2004.

Figure 1.16   Citizen views on NHS reform

government is to be applauded on its achievements here – but the under-lying managerial problems have not been addressed, and even this achievement on waiting lists will be only a temporary one (see Figure 1.18).

Another government achievement has been its drive to introduce patient choice which, again, is something that the patients and taxpayers want (see Figure 1.18).

The UK's underinvestment in medical technology was discussed earlier in this chapter, and the evidence is portrayed graphically in Figure 1.20.

The union's position that the NHS should remain a state monopoly is based on their defence of their own interests, not on what the public – who receive the service and pay for it – wants. The principle that the patient wants the best treatment and the taxpayer wants the most efficient service, no matter whether the provider is a public, private or voluntary organiza-tion, is so obviously right that it is, perhaps, the strongest argument of all

Q: How do other European health systems perform compared with your own?

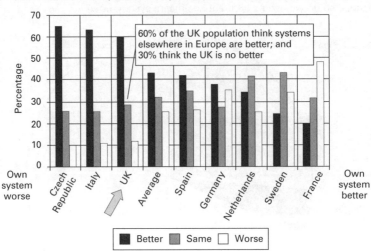

Source: Impatient for Change: European Attitudes to Healthcare Reform, Stockholm Network and Populus, 2004.

Figure 1.17 UK citizens feel there are better systems elsewhere in Europe

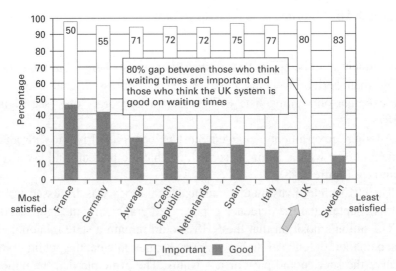

Source: Impatient for Change: European Attitudes to Healthcare Reform, Stockholm Network and Populus, 2004.

Figure 1.18 Dissatisfaction with waiting times

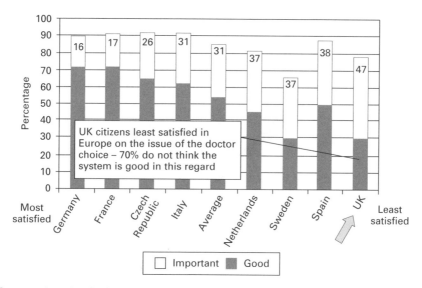

Source: *Impatient for Change: European Attitudes to Healthcare Reform*, Stockholm Network and Populus, 2004.

Figure 1.19   Dissatisfaction with choice of doctor

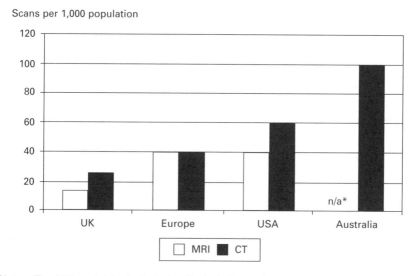

Note: The MRI market in Australia is effectively licensed and therefore demand has been controlled, with the result that more CTs are undertaken.
Source: MIA Lodestone.

Figure 1.20   UK underinvestment in medical technology

Question: Should it matter whether hospitals are run by government or the private sector as long as everyone including the least well off has access to them?

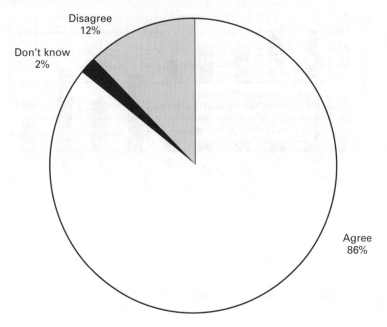

Disagree
12%

Don't know
2%

Agree
86%

Source: NHS Survey, February 2004.

Figure 1.20 Private versus public sector provision

for dismantling the NHS's monopoly. Figure 1.21 demonstrates the innate common sense of the British people.

This chapter has attempted to make the case for change. The next chapter will discuss in more depth what is wrong with the NHS, and where reform needs to be directed.

2

What is wrong with the NHS?

Key points

1 *Aneurin Bevan's founding principles of the NHS were based on patient choice and clinical freedom. Since 1948, the NHS has moved from having patients' rights at its core, to having 'Union' rights at that position.*
2 *The NHS is a centralized bureaucracy that, without fundamental reform, will continue to fail.*
3 *At the core of its failure is a dysfunctional organization and chronically poor management.*

A central argument of this book is that the reforms that the government are embarked upon (and the further recommendations of this book) will make the NHS true once more to its founding principles. Aneurin Bevan's founding principles of the NHS were based on patient choice and clinical freedom. Since 1948, the NHS has moved from having patients' rights at its core, to having 'Union' rights in that position.

Bevan's guiding principle for the NHS was service to the patients whom, he believed, should have a choice in the selection of their doctor, and no government interference with the doctor's clinical freedom.[1] State ownership was not a core principle, but a means to an end. Over 58 years later, the state-owned NHS, as a huge monolithic organization, has become seriously adrift from its customers, its payors (the taxpayers) and its founding principles.

The reason that the NHS took the form it did in 1948 was that it reflected the social necessities of the Second World War and immediate post-war period, when creating all-encompassing national organizations solved large national problems. At a time of post-war shortage, this was essential. But at the time of writing, after nearly sixty years of peace, economic and service development, a state-owned and state-run NHS is an anachronism; a relic of a previous age. As Alan Milburn, a former Minister of Health, put it:

> The NHS is a product of the era in which it was formed. In the post-War world of the mid twentieth century, big national problems were solved by creating big national institutions. Just as the National Coal Board took over a failing coal industry, so Nye Bevan's new National Health Service took over a failing health system. The NHS for the first time gave Britain a national system of Health care.

He went on to say:

> The benefits were enormous, not least in driving through public health and immunisation programmes. But as the century wore on the NHS fell behind. Cost containment took precedence over quality of care. Top down control stifled local innovation. As a monopoly provider there was no plurality in organisation and no choice for the user.[2]

Prior to the foundation of the NHS in 1948 good-quality healthcare was a privilege for those who could afford it. During the Second World War, soldiers received better medical care than they had ever received in pre-war Britain, and developed higher expectations of what they should receive in the future.

The establishment of the NHS was the result of the expectations of both the public and the new Labour government. The Emergency Medical Service and the Beveridge Report, by Lord Beveridge, a Liberal politician, formed the basis of the NHS. At this time, advances in medicine had created optimism that there were cures for a whole range of formerly incurable diseases, such as tuberculosis.

By 1948, it had become increasingly clear that the old hospital system could not continue. Voluntary hospitals, historically the only resort for most of the population, could raise only a fraction of the money they needed. When Bevan nationalized the hospitals, he faced strong opposition from the doctors (who are now holding on to the 'old NHS' as if it was their idea in the first place!). Over time, the hospital consultants became more comfortable with the new arrangements, and hospital specialists became NHS employees. In reality, they had little choice, as they needed the resources of the hospitals to practice. Bevan kept the hospital consultants sweet – he gave them the right to have private patients even in beds inside NHS hospitals or, as he put it more lyrically, 'I filled their mouths with gold'.

As reflected in the House of Commons debate on the Bill to form the NHS in 1948, most opposition to the formation of the NHS came from the British Medical Association (BMA) in general, and general practitioners in particular. General practitioners were initially opposed to the new service because they disliked the idea of not having paying patients, and they did not want to lose the right to buy and sell their practices. They also were resistant to the notion of being civil servants.

Bevan conceded that general practitioners could remain self-employed and by 5 July 1948, the first day of the NHS, nearly all the doctors had decided that they would sign up to the new system. GPs remain at the time of writing what they have always been – self-employed contractors who run small businesses sub-contracted to the NHS. However, this is not, as many claim, evidence that the private sector is already a large part of the NHS – the GPs are, in effect, salaried employees, who operate a monopoly and who think with the Civil Service's 'protectionist' and 'paternalistic' mindset. They have become what they feared.

GPs are crucial to the British healthcare system, but their political leaders in the BMA continue their conservative approach – although now they want to protect their dysfunctional monopoly. Patricia Hewitt makes the point (stretching the point, however, with regard to GPs) that a large part of our healthcare system, especially in the supplier industries, is already private sector:

> Nye Bevan recognized that there would always be some independent sector involvement in the National Health Service. GPs were – and most still are – independent contractors wholly dedicated to caring for NHS patients. High street pharmacists, opticians and most NHS dentists are self-employed professionals or small businesses. The private sector builds our hospitals and provides our equipment. More than 20% of the NHS budget goes on medicines supplied by pharmaceutical companies. And individual NHS organizations have always purchased small numbers of treatments from the private sector to keep waiting lists down. None of this was privatisation, none of it compromised the basic principles of the NHS.[3]

Although Bevan effectively nationalized hospitals in 1948, he did so as a means to an end. His core principle was not about state ownership, but that the NHS should be a free health service available to all and funded from taxation. There were three principles to the NHS:

> • Services were provided entirely free of charge at the point of use.
> • Central taxation funded the services.
> • Everyone was eligible for care.

Nothing in this book seeks to change these enduring principles – on the contrary, the wish is to see them strengthened. Bevan's objective was to give us all 'serenity' as he called it: the knowledge that we will be cared for (though regrettably not spared), when we are ill. He succeeded in creating a system of healthcare for serious medical conditions that can be used by all, free at the point of use.

A lack of reform is the real threat to Bevan's founding principles underpinning the NHS. People will choose increasingly to opt out of a failed system. The union's battle to retain their rights, and to traduce citizens' rights, is now reaching fever pitch. Strike action, which will further undermine patient safety, is increasingly threatened. The defence of their privileges is shocking:

End NHS reforms or my members may vote Tory,
warns union chief
Gordon Brown and other candidates for the Labour leadership must agree to scrap the Blairite NHS reforms to stop the Conservative Party winning the next election, the head of Britain's biggest union Unison declared yesterday, speaking on the eve of the Trades Union Congress in Brighton. The unions have a third of the votes in leadership contests. (*Daily Telegraph*, January 2006, p. 4)

The NHS worked well in its early days, in an exhausted and impoverished post-war Britain, but structurally it has become obsolete and outdated. It has become over centralized and bureaucratic – it has been taken over by the civil servants and bureaucrats.

The NHS is a centralized bureaucracy that, without fundamental reform, will continue to fail

Chambers Twentieth-Century Dictionary defines bureaucracy as 'a system of government by officials, responsible only to their departmental chiefs'. All observations on bureaucracy fit the present-day NHS. Socrates said 'the perfect bureaucrat everywhere is the man who manages to take no decisions and escape all responsibility'. Brooks Atkinson commented that 'Bureaucracy defends the status quo long past the time when the quo has lost its status.'[4]

One theme of this book is that the NHS is the first battlefield on which the citizens of the UK need to wrestle back the services for which they pay. The civil servants will defend their privileges and their incompetence vigorously. If we lose the battle for the NHS, then we run the risk of losing the battle to take back for the people the 40 per cent of the economy that is paid for by the people.

A recent MORI poll talks volumes about public perception of public services in Britain (see Figure 2.1).

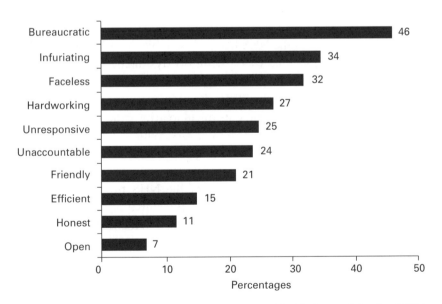

Source: Research study conducted for the Department of Health, Report, 7 October 2005 by Ben Page and Andy Byrom, MORI Social Research Institute. Survey of 2000 GB aged 18+.

Figure 2.1 Which words apply to public services in Britain these days?

At the beginning of the 1960s there was optimism in the country: economic growth seemed certain and the NHS was an admired institution. But from the mid-1960s, the economic situation deteriorated with poor balance of trade figures and severe deflation. In 1967, the pound was devalued and the third decade of the NHS began in financial crisis.

At the close of 1967, Kenneth Robinson, the Health Minister, announced that the government's views on the structure of the NHS would be set out in a Green Paper. The BMJ pressed for 'modernisation and reform' and for the integration of the management and financing of the NHS.[5]

Self-congratulatory noises from the Department of Health and Social Security (DHSS) heralded the thirtieth anniversary of the NHS, but the medical profession took a different view and dissociated itself from the celebrations:

> In 1948, the NHS may have been an example to the rest of the world, but 30 years later it measures poorly against many alternative methods of providing healthcare, and its medical and nursing staff are disillusioned and depressed. Yet only ten years ago the same staff were enthusiastic and optimistic. There is nothing wrong with the concept of the NHS . . . What has gone wrong?[6]

The problem was that the NHS had an insatiable thirst for money in the context of a bureaucracy that was structurally dysfunctional and unable to cope. As medical technology advanced, so did its costs, exacerbating the need for more NHS resources. This situation was compounded by the reluctance of successive governments to get to grips with the situation and radically reform the NHS. This state of affairs continued until 1997, when a new government, committed to putting substantial investment into the NHS, was elected.

Some of the most telling criticisms of the NHS from 1948 to 1997 come from Ken Jarrold, the former Chief Executive of County Durham and Tees strategic health authority, in his speech to the Institute of Health Management's annual conference:

> If I had to choose one phrase to describe the NHS from 1948 to 1997 it would be relative decline. Throughout this period, governments did not face up to the challenge of adequate investment in the NHS. As Derek Wanless' first report demonstrated, the NHS has been starved of resources.[7]

But Jarrold's criticisms go beyond a shortage of resources over the years:

> [it] is a service that was staff centred rather than patient centred. Towards the end of the period, this was increasingly challenged but the predominant theme was that the NHS was not primarily concerned about patient interests.
>
> Two examples – first services were often not organized for the benefit of patients. Diagnostic and treatment appointments were often unco-ordinated. There was no concept of choice; there was little attempt to empower patients to play an active part in their treatment and care. Carers were often excluded from the process.

According to Jarrold, other 'negative characteristics' include:

> The pre 1997 NHS had very long waiting times . . . The . . . characteristic of the pre 1997 NHS was an almost complete absence of service frameworks. There was little attempt to define how services for key patient groups should be delivered in accordance with best practice. Staff and patients did not have agreed pathways and standards against which to judge the services provided in their area and there were no national service frameworks . . . a lack of focus on health and a deep reluctance to discuss connections between poverty and health. The problem was that for the first 49 years of the NHS the focus and attention of most managers was on support and administrative services. Very little management attention was devoted to patient care.[8]

As has been often repeated in this book, generally, the politicians, in terms of policy and commitment to reform, are going in the right direction. But these will be undermined and negated if the core problem of the NHS – the centralized bureaucracy and poor management is not addressed. The government has to dismantle the bureaucracy (decentralize, de-bureaucratize and depoliticize); be much more radical in its commissioning policy and introduce a 'failure regime' that will create competition (in the citizens' interest) and root out poor management, beginning with the senior NHS managers who have, at best, been complicit in this failure and, at worst, its architects.

These mechanisms will make the government's reform agenda work. Without them, reform will be stillborn. The issue is not public sector versus private sector – the issue is that the NHS is a monopoly. The determined and principled behaviour of many nurses and doctors day-by-day is undermined by the organizational and management decrepitude that inevitably results from a monopoly position.

Monopolies, whether in the private or public sector are bad. They eventually let down customers and add costs (in the case of the NHS, at the expense of taxpayers). The concept of the NHS is not the enemy – abuse of monopoly power is the enemy. A strategic consultancy review in 2000 from the Virgin Group, commissioned by the Secretary of State for Health, referred to the 'dead hand of bureaucracy stifling (NHS) staff who had lost pride in their jobs'.[9] The Virgin report blamed over-centralized bureaucracy for the poor state of too many dirty hospitals, chaotic arrangements for booking treatments and a lack of consideration for patients.[10]

Unsurprisingly, but inexplicably, the NHS Confederation sees the NHS as a lean and mean machine that compares favourably with other countries' healthcare systems. As their Policy Director, Nigel Edwards, puts it:

> There are sound reasons for the increase in the number of managers, both linked to the necessary reforms taking place within the NHS, and to more general changes common to healthcare systems across the world.[11] More specifically, the NHS has been going through a period of substantial reform, which has also brought with it a significant increase in management capacity. NHS managers are overseeing the largest healthcare recruitment programme in the world, with 60,000 staff joining the service in the last year alone. Managers are responsible for modernising the pay and conditions of over a million staff through the Agenda for Change initiative, and for implementing new contracts for consultants and family doctors. They are tasked with implementing a major overhaul of the NHS IT infrastructure to enable all patients to book with a hospital of their choice. Independent assessments of the NHS have found that good management makes a vital contribution to high quality healthcare. For example, last year's Audit Commission report on progress against the NHS Plan found 'there is good evidence that better managed healthcare produces better results for patients' and that the key to improvement is better management of resources.[12]

Nigel Edwards is right: good healthcare does require good management. But the current structure, organization and the ways things are managed in the NHS appears to be accepted by many in the NHS as 'not a problem'. For them, it is just a question of throwing more managers and more money at the difficulties. The politicians, profoundly inexperienced in management, wonder why their policies do not bring improvement.

The real problem is the same as in all vast bureaucracies

In bureaucracies, local decision-making becomes enfeebled and the day-by-day objective is:

> (a) To avoid making decisions; and
> (b) To stick by the rules without questioning them.

Hidebound compliance to bureaucratic procurement rules, for example, mean that armies of people create a hugely expensive machine that obscures the issues, and delays the acquisition of goods and services that benefit the patient – and all because the major incentive for NHS administrators (and this is true for the UK public service generally), is to 'cover their backs', 'keep their noses clean', and be promoted through seniority rather than for delivering an efficient service to the public.

Not only does the NHS have too many non-value-adding administrators but, like many bureaucracies, it is extravagant in spending money on management consultants. Instances such as this one reported recently are typical:

> **Health bosses 'waste' £¹/₂ m**
> An NHS Trust with a £23million debt spent £500,000 on accountants – who advised them to cut spending. City accounting firm KPMG was called in by Selby and York Primary Care Trust after it was identified as an organization at risk of serious financial overspend last December. (*The Sun*, February 2006, p. 26)

In terms of the spending on management consultants, the figures are vague (again, a failure of financial management), but some reliable sources estimate the NHS spends as much as £1 billion per annum on management consultants.

The size of the NHS bureaucracy has always been a matter of conjecture, a worrying situation in itself, but most would agree that one in five staff (a quarter of a million people) in the NHS are administrators. The constant movement of staff around the NHS, and some staff counted, for example, as nurses but who are doing mainly administrative work, compounds the problem. This issue was recently highlighted in an *Observer* article outlining the diary of a nurse: 'Nurses are being overloaded with paperwork and administrative tasks, with as much as 40 per cent of their working week diverted from patient care.'[13]

In November 2005, the Department of Health released figures that showed that the NHS spent almost £170 million in London on management and administration in the previous financial year. According to the *Evening Standard*: Figures released by the Department of Health today show some Primary Care Trusts are paying out more than £10 million a year on bureaucrats. It is the equivalent of more than £40 for every patient and would pay for dozens of doctors and nurses.[14] Setting aside the *Evening Standard*'s 'populist' rhetoric, they make another pertinent point, that other PCTs manage to spend less than a quarter of that figure – raising suspicions that bigger spenders are wasting money.

Figures published by Monitor, the independent regulator of NHS foundation trusts, showed that University College London Hospitals (UCLH) Trust has built up the largest deficit – £17.4 million – since foundation trusts were first introduced in 2004. UCLH's response was to issue a statement blaming the opening of a new teaching hospital and the 'fallout of two terrorist incidents in July' for its financial position. Apparently, sixty-one people were treated at UCLH after the 7 July 2005 bombings, fifty of whom were reported to have minor injuries. Two-thirds of the casualties were discharged the same day.[15]

When the Audit Commission looked at payment by results in the NHS, they concluded: 'Finally, payment by results is exposing existing weaknesses in the NHS, in health economies and in individual institutions – underlying financial difficulties, inadequate financial management arrangements and problems with quality data.'[16]

Payment by results is a move in the right direction

As the OECD observed:[17]

Reforming the way budgets are allocated within the NHS, towards activity-based funding mechanisms is therefore likely to be a fruitful avenue and, the payment by results policy is a significant step in this direction . . . The experience from a number of OECD countries using activity-based funding for healthcare is that it raises activity, sometimes significantly, and thereby is a key factor for reducing waiting times . . . Moreover, reducing long waiting times via funding incentives to raise activity rather than trying to enforce waiting time guaranteed by targets, would leave more room for hospitals and doctors to take local circumstances and patients' individual needs into account . . . A recent OECD study has compared countries with and without waiting times for elective surgery and found that countries are less likely to report problems with waiting times if they rely mainly on activity-based funding for hospitals rather than mainly on fixed budgets and if they pay hospital doctors on a fee-for-service basis rather than a salary basis. The difference is statistically significant when controlling for other factors affecting supply and demand of healthcare including public and private spending, hospital capacity (number of beds), number of doctors and population age structure (Siciliani and Hurst, 2003)[18] . . . The finding . . . which shows that higher spending helps to reduce waiting times as France, Germany, Switzerland and the United States which do not report waiting times problems all spend a large share of GDP on healthcare. However, spending differences are not a sufficient explanation as for example Belgium without waiting time spends no more than Denmark, Netherlands and Australia all of which have substantial waiting time problems. What appears to be equally important is the incentives provided by funding mechanisms and none of the four countries that had mainly activity-based funding in 2000 reported waiting time problems – despite the fact that Austria and Japan have comparatively low levels of spending. For the NHS to achieve a durable reduction in waiting times, increased funding as well as improved incentives would be necessary.

The NHS budgetary system is chaotic and lacking in financial management arrangements and financial management skills. There has been a heated debate about NHS productivity; the best that can be said about it was succinctly put by Patricia Hewitt:

Statisticians argue about productivity within the health service. As we explained in a report last week, the old measures – by failing to take account of improvements in quality and the increasing number of people's lives we are saving – understated NHS productivity. But even if the real productivity growth is around 1% – as we believe – rather than negative, it needs to be far higher.[19]

Or as the OECD succinctly, but diplomatically, put it:

Policy-makers should address the following key challenges: **Ensure that public money is spent efficiently to contain the tax burden**. Increased expenditure on health and education has been accompanied by reforms aiming to ensure that resources are better used, but further improvements can be made.[20] [Bold text in original]

Although the government is trying to tackle projected deficits and increase productivity in the NHS, a lot more needs to be done, and without radical reform, the government's reform programme will peter out. This has been reiterated by a *Financial Times* analysis of Department of Health data that shows that 'the Government will miss its (waiting time) target without additional capacity and reform of the way the service operates'.[21] The journalist, Nic Timmins, goes on to say: 'But published figures show that the average wait for an outpatient appointment is currently almost 7 weeks – more than five weeks longer than the two weeks it will need to be by 2008. That figure has been falling so slowly that on current trends it will take 35 years to get down to an average two-week wait.'

Alan Maynard, Professor of Health Economics at York University, provided one explanation for this: 'To hit waiting time targets will require "an unprecedented increase in productivity", he said, when on most measures, NHS productivity has been falling as extra spending has gone into pay. For both the consultants' and GPs' contracts there has been a big increase in pay but no matching increase in productivity.'[22]

In a press release,[23] the Department of Health announced that savings of £1.7 billion had been achieved since March 2004 – £200 million ahead of target: 'I am delighted to announce that we are £200 million ahead of our target to achieve savings of £6.5 billion by March 2008.' Patricia Hewitt went on to say: 'However, these savings show that productivity gains and improved quality of care go hand in hand.'

It is clear, too, that Patricia Hewitt has become increasingly aware of the poor financial management within the NHS:

Hewitt demands more rigour in NHS investment
Patricia Hewitt is preparing tough new rules to stop hospitals in
England spending huge sums on equipment and buildings without
knowing whether they can afford to use them. (*Guardian*, February
2006, p. 11)

The inability of a substantial number of NHS Trusts to manage and
balance their books puts a big question mark over their ability to implement successfully payment by results.

It is early days for payment by results. It is evidence of poor management practice that it has taken nearly sixty years for the NHS to come up
with a cost accounting system. The opposition it regularly receives from
people within the NHS is testimony to the mindset that pervades the organization. It is true, however, that the evolution of payment by results
(PbR) needs to be managed. In particular:

- It needs to cover chronic diseases as well as acute procedures.
- It needs to be underpinned by clinical pathways over a full cycle
  of care. The importance of viewing the 'full cycle of care', and
  associated outcomes, as opposed to focusing on episodic events
  in a patient's treatment, is covered in the next chapter.
- It needs to be developed so that it encompasses both costs and
  benefits. The danger of a cost-driven payment by results is that it
  will overlook the system benefits of a higher-cost procedure. It
  could be that prescribing a higher-cost drug, or undergoing a
  higher-cost procedure will produce a better outcome for the
  patient, and/or lower costs elsewhere in the system (lower-cost
  aftercare, for example). This feature will also be encouraged by
  looking at the 'full cycle of care', as in the previous point.
- Finally, PbR needs to recognize that some environments are
  inherently higher-cost. This could be because of managers, for
  example, having to work within the constraints of a more fragmented hospital environment, or, at the other extreme, suffering
  higher depreciation costs as a result of managing within an
  expensive new environment. Those managers running large
  Private Finance Initiative (PFI) initiatives have a point when they
  urge the Department of Health to look again at the PbR tariff, and
  to create a 'level playing field' (and, to be fair, this is a factor in

UCLH's deficit) where the higher costs of PFI over traditional hospitals are reimbursed separately. Says one chief executive: 'You should take these fixed legacy costs of the estate out of the tariff.'[24]

This issue of legacy costs is an important one, and one with important managerial implications. It is a very simple principle to managers in the private sector that previous mistakes should not be allowed to prejudice the quality of decisions about the future. This concept of 'sunk cost' is not always understood by managers in the public sector. Past deficits or expensive prior decisions about building a more elaborate hospital than was truly required should not be allowed to influence decisions about how to benefit patients in the future – and how to do that cost efficiently from a taxpayer's point of view. There are numerous cases of this simple rule being overlooked in the NHS, as deficit-ridden hospitals are starved of the money they need to provide current and future services. This is another example of the poverty of modern management practice in a state-run bureaucracy.

The *Health Service Journal* reported that: 'Finance experts are examining whether changes should be made to the current NHS accounting system to prevent a type of "double counting" which can leave Trusts forecasting huge deficits.'[25]

The crux of the problem was the RAB (resource allocation and budgeting) system, which, according to the *Health Service Journal* (HSJ), creates a problem because the Department of Health reduces the local health economy's allocation by the level of deficit run up in any year. In most cases, the Strategic Health Authority recovers the money by cutting the Trust's income. However, the RAB system requires that the underlying deficit remains on the balance sheet and will only be eliminated if the organizations can swiftly cut costs or increase income. This process seems to reflect a situation where it is impossible to build an accurate picture of the real budgetary status of NHS trusts. HSJ's cartoonist, Haldane, portrays the situation with a cartoon showing two NHS managers: one holding a sign 'accountancy system to blame for deficit' and saying 'I may be lousy with figures, but I'm brilliant at excuses.'

Hostility towards RAB is reflected by Primary Care Trust (PCT) chief executives: 'They go on to to say that the introduction of . . . RAB in 2001

– variously described as "totally bizarre", "mad", "extraordinary" and "an absolute abomination" – means that those parts of the service with a historical finance problem have almost no chance of resolving it.'[26]

This type of voodoo economics is typical of bureaucracies. The objective should be to set up a system that allows managers to make informed decisions based on good data. It is quite possible that one region should go into deficit for a number of years if it has been under-invested in the past. We need to find a way of making this happen.

We know from experience that *many consultants claim that they are twice as productive in private hospitals* because the NHS is so disorganized that half the time (literally) the patient, or the patient's notes, or the theatre team are not in the theatre at the same time. Patricia Hewitt has hinted at this kind of disorganization:

> A few months ago, I met an utterly dedicated – and utterly frustrated – orthopaedic surgeon. He told me that out of the 40 hours he is paid as an NHS consultant, he spends about 6 hours actually operating. He waits while a patient is prepared and anaesthetised. He waits again after the operation until the next patient is ready. If he's lucky, he operates on two patients each morning and another one or two in the afternoon . . . You can imagine my fascination, then, when I learnt about another orthopaedic specialist, John Petri, who moved to England after working in France. Here, with twice as many surgeons and anaesthetists for about the same number of patients, he found waiting lists. In France, there were none. So he insisted on importing the French practice – organising two operating theatres in parallel, so that he doubles the number of patients he can treat.[27]

The evidence shows that the NHS has low productivity; it is unmanageable in its present form and does not give value for money.

The whole issue of NHS productivity came to light after a damning report by the Office for National Statistics (ONS), which resulted in a bad tempered response from the government:

> The ONS suggested some £6 billion a year in spending was left unimplemented through bureaucratic inefficiency. ONS researchers concluded that productivity fell between four and eight per cent since Labour came to power. Pound for pound, ONS said as much as eight per cent of the extra funds drawn from the Treasury were wasted. The

ONS found that while monies earmarked for the NHS rose from 32 to 39 per cent over an eight-year period, service output to patients increased by just 28 per cent.[28]

Productivity in the health sector has fallen consistently since 1997, according to figures published by Government statisticians on Monday. The conclusion follows six months of intensive effort by the Office for National Statistics, government departments were asked to derive the sector's first official measure of productivity. The researchers concluded that it fell between 4 and 8 per cent, depending on how it was measured, in the six years to 2003.[29]

John Reid MP, the then Health Secretary, was quick to hit back: 'It's absurd that the current measure of productivity does not cover the range of massive improvements that are being seen across the NHS.'[30]

A response also came from the Statistics Commission, which questioned the value of NHS productivity figures because they did not include 'crucial' changes in the quality of services:

The independent watchdog, which oversees the Office for National Statistics, told *Public Finance* that the methodology used to assess public sector outputs failed to give a full picture. Commission chief executive Richard Alldritt said the review by Sir Tony Atkinson of government statistics, which delivered its interim report in July [2004], had identified measures of quality as the key component of meaningful output figures. At the moment the methodology captures input and activities, such as the number of operations, but does not assess the resulting changes to the quality of services.[31]

Professor Julian Le Grand, commenting in 2005 in a *Guardian* leader, said:

The existing independent treatment centres are operating at much higher levels of productivity than comparable NHS units, and doing so with very high levels of patient satisfaction. The productivity differences may be partly explained by differences in the procedures undertaken, but this is unlikely to be the major factor.[32]

In their initial report,[33] the ONS did add some caveats:

There is further uncertainty, which is not captured in the figures. A number of shortcomings associated with the sources and methods used in compiling output figures have been identified as part of the development work to conform with the international guidelines and by the Atkinson Review of Measurement of Government Output and Productivity for the National Accounts. The most important of these are:

- The output figures do not capture quality changes;
- Data on GP contracts are derived from a household survey which does not provide accurate estimates of growth from one year to the next;
- Notwithstanding the wider coverage introduced by the new methodology in June 2004, the output estimates are still based on a subset of activities carried out by the NHS in England, and growth in these may not be representative of all activities;
- The output estimates are calculated using information from the NHS in England as a proxy for the UK; [and]
- Information systems do not necessarily reflect the most recent changes in the structure and practice in the NHS. For example, much activity that was once carried out in hospital inpatient settings is now carried out in outpatient settings or in general practice, but information systems do not yet identify the extent of this change.

Since the 2004 ONS Report, other bodies have been critical of how the NHS manages its finances:

Many NHS bodies need to improve their financial systems and financial management skills to meet the challenges of faster closing and improve their forecasting even under the existing financial regime. 2003–04 was a relatively stable year in terms of challenges facing NHS financial management but, despite this, a number of bodies found it difficult to manage resources effectively. Subsequent developments in 2004–05 and beyond mean that there will be increasing financial challenges which bodies will be expected to manage.[34]

When the Audit Commission looked at the NHS managing the financial implications of NICE guidance,[35] they found that the biggest perceived barrier to implementing both clinical guidelines and technology appraisals was lack of money. But they also identified other 'perceived' barriers:

- Lack of access to necessary resources – staff, equipment or space;
- Too much change already occurring;
- Too busy;
- Resistance to change;
- Apathy – lack of interest in implementing guidance; and
- Lack of knowledge – staff do not know that the guidance exists.

An analysis by KPMG of NHS finances[36] was even more damning:

- Across all the organizations reviewed KPMG observed slippage in the cost improvement programmes that had been introduced to help reduce spending.

In particular they noted:

- Failure to implement cost improvement programmes early enough with a lack of consideration for lead times;
- Lack of detailed implementation plans and unrealistic plans;
- Lack of ownership of plans within the organization;
- A simple assumption that savings would be delivered evenly, month by month across the year.

KPMG's point was highlighted by events at the Darvent Valley Hospital: 'this flagship hospital has been forced to ban non-emergency surgery after doctors cut long waiting lists by carrying out "too many operations" ... Surgeons performing gynaecological, urological and orthopaedic procedures have been told by local health officials that they have "over-performed".'[37]

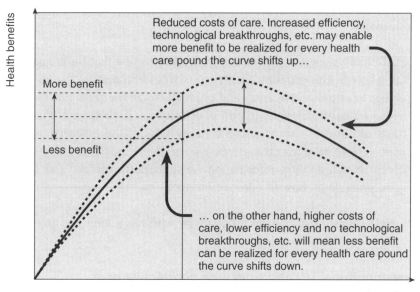

Health benefits

Reduced costs of care. Increased efficiency, technological breakthroughs, etc. may enable more benefit to be realized for every health care pound the curve shifts up...

More benefit

Less benefit

... on the other hand, higher costs of care, lower efficiency and no technological breakthroughs, etc. will mean less benefit can be realized for every health care pound the curve shifts down.

Spending

Source: King's Fund, *Spending on Health Care*, February 2006.

Figure 2.2 The importance of high levels of clinical productivity

The ONS has, subsequent to its 2004 report, published a preliminary report which they stressed was provisional and subject to 'debate and data improvements'. The report suggests that if adjustments were made for improvements such as the use of statins to treat heart attacks, productivity growth might have been about zero, rather than negative over the period: 'Taking into account the rising value of health in a growing economy, the figures suggest NHS productivity over the past five years rose by 0.9% and 1.6% annually.'[38]

Figure 2.2 illustrates the importance of high levels of clinical productivity. It also highlights the importance of cost effective use of financial resources, competent management and clinical excellence.

To date, the NHS remains on or only just above the lowest curve. This is bad for both patients and taxpayers. Worse than poor productivity is the lack of robust, useful information – rather than acres of low-value, high-cost, data – against which to manage improvement.

Many PCT chief executives recognize the importance of increased productivity:

> PCT chief executives we interviewed, who suggest that for the good of the whole health economy, acute trusts would do best to 'use as much vigour to improve efficiency and productivity in the areas that they are losing money as they are to pull in activity . . . In fact, all of the acute trusts are aware – some uncomfortably so – of the potential savings which could be released via efficiencies. What they lack, they say, is decent benchmarking information on their performance, and shared good practice on how to improve productivity.[39]

The NHS, in terms of clinical productivity, still has a long way to go.

A dysfunctional organization with chronically poor management

While the dedication of individual clinical staff within the NHS ensures that, at the moment of patient need, care is usually well delivered, those individual efforts are limited by a system that has severe defects. At the core of the dysfunctional system are well-meaning politicians, civil servants, clinicians and managers who have an impact on each other in ways that cause the dysfunction:

- *Politicians* want to see the system improved, and are appropriately responsive to news stories, opposition parties and the electorate. What happens, though, is that the politicians, who are inexperienced in management (and managing change in the NHS, with 1.4 million people, would perplex the most seasoned manager), produce knee-jerk responses, changes of policy and new initiatives that overwhelm NHS managers. And, ultimately, do not understand the impact of the dysfunctional organization and poor management – their 'experience set' is policy, and if they think things are not going well, then they introduce more policy – which inadvertently creates more dysfunction and leads to more failure. Most politicians do want to do the right thing by the British people. However, there are also well-known (within the sector) instances of overt and less benign political manipulation of the system. Keeping hospitals open (probably dangerously) in marginal constituencies has been rumoured regularly in the sector for years. Recent newspaper reports give this some credence, however. If proved right, then no greater example of the extent of dysfunctional political control is available:

Labour's scheme to 'save hospitals in marginal seats'
Emails leaked to *The Times* have led to accusations that ministers are secretly arranging to save hospitals in Labour's key marginal seats, after health secretary Patricia Hewitt ordered a meeting of senior party figures to identify areas where Labour could lose votes if hospitals were closed. Separately, it is reported that the number of casualty departments across the country could be halved, as NHS managers believe that district general hospitals can no longer cope with the pressure of providing key services such as A&E and maternity services.
(*Daily Mail*, February 2006, p. 2; *The Times*, p 1)

Labour accused of secret plan to save hospitals in key seats
The Health Secretary has been accused of ordering senior Labour figures to identify 'heat maps' showing where the party could lose votes if hospitals were closed. Opposition MPs called yesterday for a parliamentary inquiry into the behaviour of Hazel Blears, the Labour Party chairman, after *The Times* disclosed that she had been involved in the discussions about hospital closures.
(*Daily Mail*, February 2006, p. 27; *The Times*, p. 2; *Guardian*, p. 6; *Daily Telegraph*, p. 2; *Daily Express*, p. 9; *Evening Standard*, p. 4; *The Sun*, p. 2)

- The *civil servants*, who run the Department of Health, are, again, largely well-meaning public servants, but they are, once again, inadequate agents of change. There is a view, however, that the Civil Service is perhaps more wilfully opposed to change. It is easier for them, in terms of job security and lack of accountability, to maintain the monopoly, and to keep outsiders out. Not only are the incumbent managers profoundly unsuitable to lead the change process (quite simply, they are the blockages to change), but also management in the modern sense is not part of the tradition or current practice within the Civil Service. In a recent KPMG report[40] on management in Whitehall, the following was written:

> Improving efficiency requires management ... Yet go to Whitehall and ask, 'Who manages?' It's not the politicians. But neither are Whitehall's permanent secretaries, who lack the fundamental attributes required of the manager – delegated authority for which they are personally accountable. Whitehall is unmanaged. It is not realistic to expect the rest of the public sector to adopt modern management structures and incentives when the public sector's core is governed by constitutional conventions which emerged in the middle of the 19th century ... well before the management revolution that swept the private sector ... [There are] two antithetical models of the civil service:
>
> o   The management model is about management and delivery of services to users of public services. It is crisp and results-orientated. Line managers should be accountable and have authority to manage. This requires delineation of responsibility; focus on delivering objectives and a system of incentives designed to reward delivery of those objectives.
> o   The traditionalist model is about ethos and service to ministers as policy advisers. It is amorphous, collectivist and anonymous, more concerned about culture and values than results. Responsibility is shared rather than delegated.

• There are the *clinicians* who care for their patients with skill and dedication, but who have become increasingly alienated from the 'system', partly for reasons that are their responsibility, but also because they are poorly managed by NHS managers. But it would be wrong to romanticize the clinicians – they are, often, not easy people to manage, being articulate in believing that they know exactly what is wrong with the system and what needs to change, but in fact having no education or experience in such matters. But one truism of any operational environment is that if people lose control of their day-to-day tasks, then they become hugely demotivated and disaffected. This truism applies from government ministers and senior management all the way down to cleaners and orderlies. It is this loss of control that clinicians complain about. Whether it is top-down manuals that 'de-skill' them, or disorganized operational management, bureaucratic paperwork, or mindless 'health and safety' regulations that in fact – and clearly in the eyes of clinicians – are a danger to health and safety, all of these things prevent the clinicians from dealing efficiently with their patients. And the one thing that clinicians really do care about – the reason why they chose this career – is patients. Doctors have never been more seriously disaffected from the NHS – and that is the ultimate, and most dangerous, proof of poor management.

- There are some good *NHS managers* who could hold their own in the private sector – but they are few. And even they are confounded by the dysfunctional system dynamics that the four groups – politicians, civil servants, clinicians and NHS managers – discussed set up between themselves. These dynamics are illustrated in Figure 1.5 on page 14.

The major theme of this book is that this vicious spiral has to be interrupted – and that can only be done by bringing in competent management.

Some might claim that this is not, in fact, a management problem. All the evidence in the private sector points to the overriding importance of management skill as against extraneous factors, such as declining markets, government regulation or whatever. The central importance of management is demonstrated in work by the US-based Health Care Advisory Board.[41]

They examined sixty case studies where hospitals or healthcare economies had reached a financial crisis (although they did not measure clinical outcomes, it is likely that the poor management that results in financial crises also prejudices the quality of care). Their 'root cause' analysis showed that only 13 per cent of the causes were related to 'uncontrollable factors' (which indicates that 87% of the factors were controllable); that is, factors outside the control of management. This figure of 13 per cent largely comprised commercial competition which, of course, exists in the USA but not in the UK. So even in the USA (and the figure will be even higher in the UK, given that there is no competition), nearly 90 per cent of the causes of failure are under the control of management. Furthermore, in the USA, many of these factors were again driven by competition and the lack of responsiveness of managers. The second biggest category within the 87 per cent (controllable factors) for example, was misperception of new business opportunities (responding to changing epidemiology more slowly than the competitors). This category will probably not cause financial crisis in the UK – but it will, and probably has, denuded the service to UK patients. The point is that the managerial challenges in the UK are a lot easier because of the lack of competition (no consequences for poor decisions that damage patient outcomes and waste taxpayers' money), but notwithstanding that, there is chronic and widespread mismanagement.

The list of management failings in the Advisory Board study are interesting not only because they point to the central importance of management rather than factors outside of management's control: they are also interesting because they provide a blueprint for the types of management competencies that the NHS should be seeking (and generally these will be found not in the failed NHS but in managers in the private sector). This chapter concludes by looking briefly at the Advisory Board analysis, and by looking at the need for sophisticated management of the psychological challenges of working within the NHS.

Modern management in the private sector – in order to earn the right to deliver goods and services to consumers – has had to learn to improve performance by managing the root causes of failure. The Advisory Board found that 87 per cent of the root causes of failure were related to factors under management's control. They split these into two parts – 47 per cent explained by strategic failings; and 40 per cent by organizational failings. Of the strategic failings, causality was broken down further:

- 13 per cent (as described above) because of the misperception of new business opportunities (or changing epidemiology);
- 11 per cent caused by senior management distraction because of a lack of prioritization. This is probably an even bigger problem

in the UK where the dynamics described in the core diagnosis of the NHS problem creates a hugely distracting and distracted environment for NHS managers;
- 11 per cent caused by failure to exit underperforming strategies. There is probably a more basic problem in the NHS, where the fundamental management discipline of formulating strategy (designing cost-effective strategies around customer needs) is barely known;
- 6 per cent because of misperception of new business threats – which again, NHS managers are protected from in the non-competitive UK system; and
- 6 per cent a result of underinvestment in the core through a lack of understanding of customer needs.

Of the 40 per cent in organizational factors, causality was further broken down thus:

- 15 per cent resulting from a culture of conservatism, including factors such as unwillingness to make unpopular decisions, and reluctance to contradict past decisions;
- 10 per cent related to inadequate performance measurement (this barely exists at all in the NHS);
- 8 per cent caused by excessive executive turnover, meaning that there is no strategic or operational continuity;
- 4 per cent because of lack of accountability, including such factors as no business unit goals, failure to track business unit performance, and lack of performance incentives (again, this area is profoundly poor in the NHS); and
- 3 per cent caused by ineffective organizational design, by which is meant cumbersome decision-making and governance processes.

A look at these factors makes one feel it is a wonder that any service is delivered at all in the NHS. The fact that it is, and this is a major theme of this book, is through the dedication of clinicians *in spite of* the mismanagement from politicians to frontline managers.

/essure on the clinicians, and the lack of good management,
es this brief section on the psychology of management in the
are system. There are two central themes – the first is that clinicians in the healthcare system are subjected to much higher levels of
stress than in other sectors; and the failure of good management makes
this even worse. The second is that large bureaucracies such as the NHS
create a sense of 'hopelessness' which erodes management effectiveness.
The results of some research on this topic were reported recently in *The
Times*:

NHS career path is a short one

Politics and policy change, short-termism and an inability to make a
difference are among the worst things about working in the NHS,
according to a survey of health service management trainees. (*The
Times*, January 2006, *Public Agenda*, p. 6)

First, on the topic of stress in the healthcare system: nurses and doctors
have been shown to have among the highest burnout rates of any occupa-
tional groups (Schaufeli, 1999).[42] The study suggests that this is a feature
of environments that require caring and supportive behaviours. Research
suggests that the people who suffer burnout: (a) have personalities that
find it hard to cope; and (b) work in poorly managed environments.
Specifically identified in this research are factors such as lack of participation in decisions and lack of autonomy. These are two prominent
features of NHS managerial failure. It is a reasonable conclusion that poor
NHS management is contributing to higher stress levels among clinicians
– and that, by definition, poor NHS managers are incompetent to turn
things around – they are the problem, not the solution.

An apt conclusion to this chapter is a quote from the Leatherman and
Sutherland report on quality in the NHS. They identify some of the
cultural attributes of the health service:

- 'A paternalistic relationship between professional and patient'
  (Brown, 1998);
- 'Strong subcultures, both within and between professional'
  groups (Harrison and Pollitt, 1994; Degeling *et al.*, 1998);
- 'Work patterns that are task-oriented, rather than patient-
  oriented' (Joss and Kogan, 1995);

- 'Medical models of care rather than holistic patient-centred approaches' (Joss and Kogan, 1995);
- 'Power concentrated at the top and dominated by government'; and
- 'Low levels of staff morale' (Finlayson, 2002).[43]

Chapter 4 describes how and where the dysfunctional system needs to be punctured. The next chapter discusses, at some length, a vision for the NHS – a vision that is currently lacking and is urgently needed in order to mobilize those parts of the healthcare community who do want to produce a better healthcare environment for UK citizens.

3

A vision for the NHS

Key points

1 *The Labour government's policy agenda is largely moving along the right lines. However, there are some important areas where it needs to be developed.*

2 *The most important of these areas is that it requires a compelling vision that will give key participants the excitement and resolve to carry reform forward.*

3 *The timely work of Professor Michael Porter in the USA provides the elements of this vision:*

   3.1 *A relentless focus on **patient value**, based on high quality clinical outcome data; and*

   3.2 *Unrestrained competition so that the best provider earns the right to serve the patient.*

4 *In the UK, commissioners will be the crucial market-makers who will ensure that competition results in a patient-centred system.*

Refinements to the current policy agenda

Most pieces of the policy agenda have been put in place by the government. There are many adjustments required, and much play-testing and piloting, but the general thrust is right. Most of this chapter will discuss the vision for the NHS, but there are seven areas of policy that do need immediate attention:

1. Primary care has been overlooked so far. The reforms required in this area are discussed in the next chapter.

2. Integration of the healthcare system with the social care system has been neglected. Research shows that citizens are perplexed by the poor integration between these two services. This topic is also dealt with in the section on primary care in the next chapter.

3. Similarly, commissioning should be at the very core of reform, but it has been the 'dog that didn't bark', and has to become a top priority. Again, this is discussed in more detail in the next chapter.

4. The 'Connecting for Health' IT programme has to work. It is a vital engine for generating and analysing the clinical and economic information that is so sorely lacking at present.

5. There are some significant inconsistencies in policy at the time of writing – and greater consistency is required to make sure that policies are not discredited. The most obvious one is the tension between PbR, which incentivizes managers to pull volume into their hospitals, and the Out-of-Hospital White Paper, which advocates less activity in hospitals, and more treatment in the community. The work of Bill McCarthy within the Department of Health (DH) has been very good – he has given much more coherence to the policy agenda. But there is a further need to model policy in such a way that the inconsistencies can be better identified and corrected.

6. The policy agenda has prevously concentrated too much on the acute care agenda. Not only has the primary care sector been neglected, but so too has chronic disease. This has not only been a problem for patients, but has also alienated some clinicians. The majority of doctors and nurses are not doing high-profile operations, they are treating people with chronic diseases such as diabetes – and spend most of their time with the disadvantaged (who have a series of mutually reinforcing diseases) and older people. The bulk of NHS money goes into this area. Many clinicians have felt that the focus on waiting lists for acute procedures has been gimmicky. The government needs to turn serious attention to the area of chronic disease.

7. Finally, the policy agenda is (and certainly comes over as being) dry and technical. The lack of a really compelling vision that people can see is worth fighting for does two things: it makes the policy debate seem technocratic; and it 'gives all the good

tunes to the devil' in the sense that the reactionary unions (doctors, nurses and Unison) can scaremonger and misrepresent with shouts of 'privatization' and 'job losses' without a compelling counter-argument being made – and that argument is that a system is being transformed from one that has served the unions to one that serves the patient and taxpayer. It is as if an exciting trip to some great place is being organized – a holiday in some exotic resort – but instead of describing the place, the technical details of the taxi that will take the party to the airport and the aerodynamics of flight are described. We need to make sure that the aeroplane flies – but we also need to get people excited about the destination. The rest of this chapter outlines that exciting destination.

Introduction to Michael Porter's work

Recent work by the distinguished Harvard Business School professor, Michael Porter, has come at just the right moment. In wrestling with the failure of the US system, he has painted a vivid picture of where we can take the NHS in the UK – if we introduce the reforms outlined in this chapter.

Michael Porter has been a major contributor to management theory and practice for nearly thirty years. In the early 1980s, he produced groundbreaking work on corporate and competitive strategy[1], which still provides the standard approach to business strategy in most organizations. He then wrote a hugely influential book, *Competitive Advantage of Nations*,[2] which outlines why countries are competitive in producing some goods and services and not others. This work has become the blueprint for industrial policy in most countries of the world. I draw on this work in Chapter 5, when I discuss how the UK can regain its international competitiveness in healthcare and biomedical science. Porter then worked on issues of competition in society; his work on regenerating depressed inner city areas becoming a touchstone for policy in this area. His latest book, *Redefining Healthcare*,[3] is going to have a huge impact on healthcare policy and practice throughout the world.

Porter embarked on his work as a result of a paradox. In all his experience, competition produced better outcomes for customers and citizens.

However, the US healthcare system seemed to have a lot of competition, but it produced a high-cost and low-quality system that did not benefit patients. The US healthcare system faces staggering performance challenges in both cost and quality because of *a failure of competition*: costs are spiralling; quality problems persist; inexplicable gaps in cost and quality exist for the same type of care across providers and geographic areas; the best providers are not rewarded, weaker providers do not go out of business; and technological innovation diffuses slowly.

Getting the right sort of competition

So healthcare in the USA is failing not because there is a *lack* of competition, but because competition takes place at the wrong levels and on the wrong things. The problem with competition in the USA is, first, that competition takes place around health plans rather than healthcare outcomes; and, second, there is a 'zero-sum' mentality whereby system participants compete to divide value, not add to or create it. They do this by:

- Shifting costs (for example, from employers to employees; from health plans to providers; from government to the private sector) without fundamentally reducing them.
- Increasing bargaining power through scale, without improving health results or efficiency.
- Capturing patients and restricting choices, thereby further limiting competition on costs and patient value.
- Reducing costs by restricting services, thereby shifting costs to patients or rationing care.

Their choices drive a vicious cycle of dysfunctional competition that ultimately:

- Makes healthcare a commodity.
- Stresses short-term 'quick-hit' cost reductions.
- Obscures true costs.
- Discourages patients from seeking the best value care.

- Shields local providers from regional or national competition.
- Promotes breadth of provider services above depth of expertise and true excellence.
- Suppresses information on health outcomes.
- Perpetuates the myth that all providers provide equally well.

The consequences include erosion of quality; inefficiency; excess capacity; rising administrative costs; skewed incentives all around; stifled innovation; extreme fragmentation of care; and proliferating malpractice suits.

Although the UK healthcare system is poles apart from the US system, the results are astonishingly similar. A monolithic bureaucracy with no competition creates a top-down system that is, in a systems sense, unresponsive to customers. There is no incentive to publish data on health outcomes, there is no incentive for clinical teams to take their expertise out of their local area, and a (poorly managed) cost-driven system is involved in periodic bouts of cost-cutting. The UK system is completely different from the US system, but by being systems that, for different reasons, do not have **patient value** as the core engine of their dynamics, they are very similar in their failure.

In the USA, efforts to reform healthcare have failed because they have not addressed the nature of competition through the system. Rather, their focus has been fixed in turn on costs, regulation, health plan choice, and provider and hospital practices.

Porter forestalls the wrong conclusion – that what is needed in response to a failing US healthcare system is an NHS-type system:

It simply strains credibility to imagine that a large government entity would streamline administration, simplify prices, set prices according to true costs, help patients make choices based on excellence and value, establish value based competition at the provider level and make politically neutral and tough choices to deny patients and reimbursement to sub-standard providers ... The real solution is not to make health insurance a government monopoly or to make all physicians government employees but to open up value based competition on results at the right level. (Porter and Teisberg, *Redefining Healthcare*, p. 89).[4]

The only way to transform healthcare is through value-based competition on results, a 'positive-sum' competition from which all system participants can benefit:

The way to transform healthcare is to realign competition with value for patients. Value in healthcare is the health outcome per dollar of cost expended. If all system participants have to compete on value, value will improve dramatically. As simple and obvious as this seems to be, however, improving value has not been the central goal of the participants in the system. The focus instead has been on minimising short-term costs and battling over who pays what. The result is that many of the strategies, organisational structures and practices of the various actors in the system are badly misaligned with value for the patient. (Porter and Teisberg, *Redefining Healthcare*, p. 4).

Value-based competition is guided by eight principles (Porter and Teisberg, *Redefining Healthcare*, p. 98):

1. The *focus should be on value* (the health outcome per dollar (or £) of cost expended) *for patients* (not for health plans, hospitals, doctors or employers), and lowering not just on costs.
2. *Competition must be based on results*, defined as *patient health outcomes* per unit of cost at the medical condition level. This is **patient value**. Ensuring that providers compete to be excellent and earn their right to practice is the only way to create incentives for rapid and widespread improvement, and it is the only cure for medical errors, under-treatment (for the uninsured in the USA or the more disadvantaged people in the UK who are less pushy than the middle classes), and over-treatment (as, mainly in the USA, providers try to maximize revenue and avoid malpractice suits by advising patients to have every diagnostic test available, and to undergo procedures 'just to be on the safe side'). Staying abreast of best practices should be mandatory; sub-standard approaches would become apparent; and the effort devoted to improving care delivery structures and methods would increase dramatically.
3. *Competition should centre on particular medical conditions* (for example, diabetes, stroke, chronic kidney disease) *over the full cycle of care* (that is, prevention, diagnosis, treatment,

rehabilitation, management). Only at this level can value and results be measured in a meaningful, accurate way. Managing a full cycle of care instead of separate treatments offers far greater potential for value improvement. Providers should organize themselves around medical conditions (not by discrete special-ties and skills) in 'integrated practice units' (IPUs), which include all the necessary services for a given medical condition and are housed in dedicated facilities. The concept of organiz-ing around the 'full cycle of care', and 'integrated practice units' is illustrated in Figure 3.1, which maps out the 'cycle of care' (the Care Delivery Value Chain – CDVC) for the treatment of breast cancer.

4. *High-quality care should be less costly*, because quality and cost will improve simultaneously. Eliminating mistakes, getting it right the first time, and providing the right treatment to individ-ual patients improves outcomes, speeds recovery and reduces the need for extra treatment. The huge costs of poor diagnosis, on the other hand, are wasted or lead to inappropriate treatment, a greater risk of complications, repeat visits, and the delay of appropriate care.

5. *Value must be driven by provider experience, scale, and learn-ing at the medical condition level.* The combined effects of these drive a virtuous circle in healthcare delivery whereby providers who concentrate their effort on deeper penetration in a given medical condition will deliver the most value and innovate the most rapidly. Experience leads to skilled teams with faster rates of learning; scale allows for dedicated teams, tailored facilities, valuable feedback loops, and a critical mass of cases for learn-ing. This virtuous cycle is illustrated in Figure 3.2.

6. *Competition should be regional and national, not just local.* The outdated local bias in healthcare undermines the delivery of value, not least because of significant variations in outcomes and costs across geographical borders. No single institution needs to provide every service; patients should seek the excel-lent care that best meets their needs, wherever this may be. Providers must be encouraged not to reach minimum standards of acceptability for every medical condition, but rather to grow in their areas of expertise by competing with the best providers

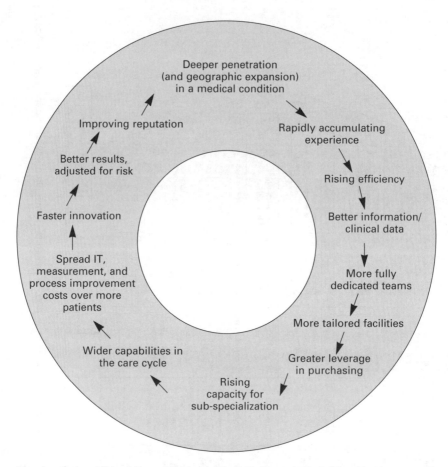

Source: Porter, Michael E. and Teisberg, Elizabeth Olmsted, *Redefining Healthcare*, p. 7. Reprinted by permission of Harvard Business School Press from *Redefining Healthcare: Creating Value-Based Competition on Results*.

Figure 3.2   The virtuous circle in treating a medical condition

anywhere and building relationships with regional, national and international centres to learn the highest standards of value, and tap into hitherto inaccessible economies of scale and experience.

7. *Results information* (that is, objective knowledge on patient outcomes and costs over a care cycle) *to support value-based competition must be widely available*. Without it, providers have no motivation or insight for improving their practice, and referring physicians and patients have no basis for decision-making. Mandatory results measurement, above all else, is the

best way to eliminate sub-standard care in the system, and the single most important step in healthcare reform:

> Mandatory measurement and reporting of results is perhaps the single most important step in reforming the healthcare system. Instead of measuring and competing on results, efforts to improve healthcare delivery have made the fundamental error of attempting to control supply and micromanage provider practices ... The whole process-oriented approach is misguided. Standardised process guidelines belie the complexity of individual patient circumstances, and freeze care delivery processes rather than foster innovation ... What is needed is to migrate patients to the truly excellent providers, which feeds a virtuous circle of provider value improvement through greater scale, better efficiency, deeper experience, faster learning, and more dedicated teams and facilities at the medical condition level. In contrast, the lift all boats model perpetuates the vicious circle where many subscale providers lack the capabilities to achieve true excellence. (Porter and Teisberg, *Redefining Healthcare*, p. 7)

8. *Innovations that increase value must be strongly rewarded.* The importance of innovation in healthcare is no different from that in other industries: it is fundamental to value improvement, but has not been rewarded and, even worse, has been viewed with unjustified suspicion. The many forms of innovation include not only technological advances, but also new types of strategies, facilities, processes and partnerships. While clinical trials (with necessary improvements) will continue to be an important vehicle for innovation, risk-adjusted results-based studies of large patient populations over extended periods of time will be of even greater value in enabling researchers to analyse and understand the effects of variations across medical conditions, treatments and outcomes. Again, the availability of results information is critical.

In healthcare, the power of market principles is greater, not less, than in most other industries. Value-based competition on results presents huge, untapped opportunities to drive care that is both of better quality and less expensive. In both the USA and the UK, it will require significant changes by all system participants. In fact, the chances of the UK creating the type of dynamics that Porter espouses are higher than for the USA. The task in the UK is to move from a monolithic, centralized system to one that focuses on **patient value** through the exercise of competition. Ironically, this centralized system has the power to engineer this new market economy by, in particular, putting commissioners in place who will, in effect, become market-makers. The opponents of change in the UK are the ideologues of the left and the public-sector unions – but their power will weaken in the face of patients demanding choice on the back of good and available information. In the USA, in contrast, the vested commercial interests are so strong that opposition will be much more difficult to overcome.

In his book, Porter goes on to outline what each of the system partici-pants needs to do in order to contribute to productive change. He explains that the providers, as the central actors in the healthcare system, will ulti-mately determine how much value is delivered in the practice of medicine and the care of patients. The primary goal and guiding compass for every healthcare provider should be excellence in **patient value**. This sounds self-evident, but in reality has been clouded by a variety of factors, and hampered by tradition. The current strategies, organizational structures and operating practices of providers are misaligned with value: the breadth of services is too broad, the approach to service delivery too narrow and un-integrated, and the geographical focus and behavioural orientation too localized.

Moving to 'positive-sum' competition on results is the only way to compete on value, which must be measured and built up medical condi-tion by medical condition, and assessed relative to peers. Imperial College Medical School and Harvard Business School have begun to collaborate with Porter to set up a 'library' of outcome measurement in the UK. Providers who take the lead on developing value-based strate-gies can act as a powerful catalyst for change throughout the system, and stand to gain immense benefits from improving the value of the health-care they deliver. Some providers in the USA are already doing so. An example is taken from the Boston Spine Group based in Massachusetts (see Figure 3.3).

OUTCOMES		METHODS

Patient Outcomes
(*before and after treatment, multiple times*)

Visual Analog Scale (pain)

Owestry Disability Index, 10 questions (function ability)

SF-36 Questionnaire, 36 questions (burden of disease)

Length of hospital stay

Time to return to work or normal activity

Service Satisfaction
(*periodic*)

Office visit satisfaction metrics (10 questions)

Overall medical satisfaction

('Would you have surgery again for the same problem?')

Medical Complications

Cardiac
  Myocardial infarction
  Arrhythmias
  Congestive heart
  failure
Vascular deep venous thrombosis
Urinary infections
Pneumonia
Post-operative delirium
Drug interactions

Surgery Complications

Patient returns to the operating room
Infection
Nerve injury
Sentinel events (wrong site surgeries)
Hardware failure

Surgery Process Metrics

Operative time
Blood loss
Devices or products used

Source: Porter, Michael E. and Teisberg, Elizabeth Olmsted, *Redefining Healthcare*, p. 185. Reprinted by permission of Harvard Business School Press from *Redefining Healthcare: Creating Value-Based Competition on Results*.

Figure 3.3   Boston Spine Group: clinical and outcome information collected and analysed

How it would work in the UK, and how providers would compete

The vision for the UK would be that commissioners, the dispensers of public money (raised by taxes), would tender for 'natural monopoly' services (such as A&E) in a region (although, over time, there will be fewer 'natural' monopolies, and there is no reason why A&E services should not also be competitive). Excellent clinical units – the Royal Brompton, for example, in cardiovascular disease, and Great Ormond Street in paediatrics – would become national providers able to codify their expertise, and refresh it as a result of the greater caseload that they treat. They would, therefore, out-perform other clinical units, which would either be absorbed into Royal Brompton UK (and, eventually,

International, bringing invisible earnings into the UK) and benefit from best practice, or be replaced by Royal Brompton UK clinicians. Hospitals would become facility management businesses, allowing franchises (such as Royal Brompton UK in cardiovascular disease, and Great Ormond Street UK in paediatric services) to operate in their facility.

More broadly, Porter argues, value-based competition has eight imperatives for providers. These are the strategies that the successful clinical units would pursue, and apply just as much in the UK setting than in the USA. They are the imperatives that a unit like Royal Brompton UK would pursue:

1. *Redefine the business around medical conditions*, the basic unit of analysis for thinking about value in healthcare. Every provider must define the set of patient-centred medical conditions in which it participates (for example, not cardiology, but congestive heart failure; not nephrology, but chronic kidney disease), and locate where it fits in the care cycle.
2. *Choose the range and types of services provided.* Broader is not better in healthcare delivery, and today's inefficient division of labour is far from ideal. Providers must pursue excellence and deepen penetration in their chosen medical conditions (*not* hyper-specialization) by making a strategic choice about what services to offer. These choices feed a virtuous circle of value in care delivery and trigger a cascade of benefits.
3. *Organize around medically-integrated practice units (IPUs).* Healthcare delivery today is highly fragmented across the care cycle. IPUs (such as the Cleveland Clinic, a US example Porter uses) are patient-centred and results-driven. They are designed around the integration of care for a medical condition, rather than a collection of discrete services, treatments or tests, and ideally have dedicated teams and facilities. They accept responsibility for the full cycle of care, even if they do not control all of it directly.
4. *Create a distinctive strategy in each practice unit.* Individual providers within each IPU should seek a distinctive and differentiating approach – for example, the delivery of superior value in specific aspects of the care cycle, or for some meaningful group of patients – that deepens the overall competence of the group. This pursuit will drive innovation and deepen expertise.

5. *Measure results, experience, methods and patient attributes by practice unit.* The ethos of secrecy in healthcare is deeply ingrained. Value can only be improved, however, when providers measure results, collect and act on clinical information, assemble comparative information, and make that information transparent.

6. *Move to single bills and new approaches to pricing.* This applies most directly to the USA. But as PbR becomes widespread in the UK, then the 'imperative' will apply equally in Britain. It is important, as was discussed in the previous chapter, that PbR applies to the full 'cycle of care', so that trade-offs that maximize **patient value** can be identified and acted upon. The current billing model undermines value by obscuring costs. The relevant unit of cost for assessing the value delivered is not a discrete service, but an episode of care and, eventually, a full care cycle. Providers who move proactively to align their practice with value will not only serve patients better, but also prosper as competition on value grows.

7. *Market services based on excellence, uniqueness and results.* Marketing must shift from breadth and institutional reputation to practicing unit excellence and value in particular medical conditions. General claims should give way to the dissemination of information relevant to patient value: experience, expertise, methods and results over full care cycles.

8. *Grow locally and geographically in areas of strength.* Growth strategies should be centred on practice units, not broad-line institutions. Geographical expansion in distinctive IPUs will offer most providers huge, untapped growth opportunities (for example, via geographical integration models for rural hospitals, remote medicine approaches, telemedicine technologies, consulting/shared services network models, and IPU management/partnership contracts for co-located facilities).

Source: Porter and Teisberg, *Redefining Healthcare*, p. 157.

Health plans and commissioning

Health plans are the fundamental building blocks of the US system. In his book, Porter talks about how they need to be reformed. Much of this is not relevant to the UK context, but in that I am advocating in this book that commissioning is developed much more fully as a major 'market-maker' in the system, then a fair amount of what Porter writes about Health Plans – and in particular how they would look in their reformed character – is directly relevant to the commissioning model that we need to build in the UK.

In the USA, Porter argues, health plans are uniquely positioned to play important value-adding roles, but they are perhaps the least trusted and most vilified actors in the system. This contrasts with the UK, where our equivalent of health plans – commissioning – can start from a clean sheet of paper, and very early on align the function to patient interests. In contrast, health plans in the USA have been around for a long time, and their strategies have increased bureaucracy and administrative costs, restricted physician choice and services to patients, and generally interfered with the delivery of value through adversarial relationships with providers and members. Their attempts to shift costs, micromanage providers and treat healthcare as a commodity have not only reinforced 'zero-sum' competition but also failed to control spiralling costs. Health plans can and must, Porter argues, dispense with their current culture of denial and second-guessing, and reorientate their approach around value-based competition.

Their fundamental role must be to help members improve their health by enabling choice and the management of health; measuring and rewarding providers based on results; maximizing the value of care over the full care cycle; minimizing administrative transactions and simplifying billing; and competing on members health results. These objectives, and they translate very well into objectives for commissioners in the future UK system, require that health plans:

- Provide health information and support to patients and physicians/clinicians.
- Organize around medical conditions, not geography or administrative functions.
- Develop measures and assemble results information on providers and treatments.
- Actively support and enable (not restrict) provider and treatment choice with information and unbiased counselling.
- Organize information and patient support around the full cycle of care.

- Provide comprehensive disease management and prevention services to all members, even healthy ones.
- Restructure the health plan/commissioner–provider relationship.
- Shift the nature of information sharing with providers.
- Reward provider excellence and value-enhancing innovation for patients.
- Move to single bills (or tariffs in the UK system) for episodes and cycles of care, and single prices.
- Simplify, standardize, and eliminate paperwork and transactions.
- Redefine the health plan–subscriber relationship.
- Move to multiyear subscriber contracts and shift the nature of plan contracting.
- End cost-shifting practices, such as re-underwriting, that erode trust in health plans and breed cynicism.
- Assist in managing members' medical records.

Source: Porter and Teisberg, *Redefining Healthcare*, p. 239.

While it may seem utopian to suggest that health plans gauge their success by health results rather than costs, a growing number in the USA are already moving in these new directions. Aligning the interests of health plans/commissioners, patients, providers and plan sponsors will generate enormous consequences in terms of creativity, innovation and healthcare value. As with providers, health plans that move early will, Porter argues, gain the greatest benefits. Suppliers/providers and consumers will benefit by moving to value-based thinking, while catalysing and speeding systemic transformation. Porter maps out their key roles (Porter and Teisberg, *Redefining Healthcare*, ch. 7).

Suppliers/providers

Many suppliers have perpetuated and reinforced zero-sum competition at the expense of value for patients in their pursuit of bargaining power, their emphasis on volume, and their organization around discrete products rather than around full-care cycles. Their practices have not only failed to address patient value, but are bad strategies for the suppliers themselves.

To move to value-based competition, suppliers must:

- Compete on delivering unique value over the fully cycle of care (for example, by situating their products within a Core Delivery Value Chain (CDVC)).
- Demonstrate value based on a careful study of long-term results and costs (for example, via patient registries, 'post-approval' testing, comparative information, new relationship models with providers, health plans, and patients).
- Ensure that products are used by the right patients (for example, with less of an emphasis on the size of 'overall' markets and more delineation of patient attributes *vis-à-vis* particular treatments).
- Ensure that products are embedded in the right care delivery processes (for example, by assisting with effective product usage).
- Build marketing campaigns based on value, information and customer support.
- Offer support services that add value rather than reinforce cost-shifting.

Consumers

Consumers should be the ultimate beneficiaries of value, yet they are often uninformed and passive participants in their healthcare. Consumer choice is not an end in, and of, itself. The goal is to increase dramatically the value of care delivered, and the systemic transformation necessary to achieve this goal involves much more than just customer choice.

Consumers wield influence not by micromanaging their own care, but from acting responsibly and setting high expectations for results so that other actors in the system do their jobs well. Consumers can enable and support value-based competition by participating actively in managing personal health; expecting relevant information and seeking advice; making treatment and provider choices based on results and values, not convenience or amenities; choosing a health plan based on value added; building a long-term relationship with an excellent health plan (instead of plan churning and switching); and acting responsibly (instead of shifting costs to others in society).

The fundamental flaw in US (and UK) healthcare policy is a lack of focus on **patient value**. The US government has lacked an overall framework and focused almost exclusively on cost control and shifting costs to the private sector. Attempts at reform have been piecemeal, reactive and incremental. The result is a highly controversial system with almost 46 million uninsured people. A government-controlled national healthcare system, a single-payer system, a consumer-driven system, and various other models, have strong advocates; but none of them is a real solution, as exemplified by increasing problems in government-run health systems elsewhere.

Fortunately, the US government is not, Porter argues, the key to healthcare reform (change will come from within the system), but reform will not be complete unless government establishes the infrastructure and rules that enable value-based competition against results. Only through harnessing the power of competition can value rise and innovation flourish, to the benefit of every single participant in the system.

Porter concludes:

Moving to value-based competition on results has huge implications for any country's healthcare system, regardless of its starting point. While other advanced countries have historically boasted lower costs, they are now facing accelerated rates of cost increase and alarming quality problems similar to those in the U.S. There is growing recognition around the world of the need to refocus on value, introduce competition into state-dominated programs, rethink how providers are organized, and collect and disseminate results (Porter and Teisberg, *Redefining Healthcare*, p. 375).

Mike Porter's approach provides a rich framework that can very well be adapted to the UK's situation. In doing so, it creates a compelling vision that will give an overwhelming and indisputable justification for the reform programme.

4

Breaking the dysfunctional dynamics

Key points

1   The core problem of the NHS is the dysfunctional organizational dynamics and chronically poor management.
2   This is a self-reinforcing, and therefore very stable, system.
3   Experience of change management shows that such a system needs to be punctured at a number of points simultaneously if the behaviours and culture are to be changed.
4   There are four things that need to happen:
    4.1   The system needs to be:
          4.1.1   De-bureaucratized;
          4.1.2   Decentralized; and
          4.1.3   Depoliticized.
    4.2   Demand-side mechanisms need to be introduced and extended – patient choice is one of these, but more importantly there is a need for much more extensive measurement and publication of clinical outcomes. Patient choice can only be a really powerful mechanism for change (in fact, in the sense of 'people power', an irresistible force for productive change) if there is accessible information on which to base good choice, and unrestrained competition so that there is a supplier consequence to patient choice. Commissioning needs to be pushed up the policy agenda – it is the single most important issue. Primary care is the part of the system that most patients encounter, and it is a crucial diagnostic 'portal' into treatment for more acute conditions. The government has begun to turn its attention to commissioning and primary care – but it needs to move both further and faster.
    4.3   Competition needs to be introduced.

> 4.4 *This is a massive and complex change programme. Senior civil servants/NHS managers are, at best, complicit in living within this failed system, and at worst (especially senior managers) they are architects of the system itself. Not only do they have little interest in changing the system (a system that they have 'learnt' and a system that values their bureaucratic skills, evidenced by their rise to the top), but they have no experience of change on this scale, having spent thirty or forty years in a static state monopoly.*
>
> 5 *A recent report co-ordinated by the King's Fund points to the actions required if a patient-centred healthcare market is to develop in the UK.*

My recommendations from this diagnosis are that the vicious circle has to be punctured, simultaneously, at the following points (see Figure 4.1).

The system needs to be de-bureaucratized, decentralized and depoliticized

De-bureaucratize

A core feature of bureaucracies is that they are top-down and centrally driven. The numbers of people at the centre tend to grow in an inverse proportion to the effectiveness of the centre. Power and status within a bureaucracy are measured by the number of staff reporting to a given individual: so senior bureaucrats arrange the hierarchy so that more and more people are reporting to them – and they fight very hard to keep their 'empires'.

The early years of a new bureaucracy, however, are often quite lively – people are motivated positively by being powerful actors in the 'public good'. This was true of the NHS in its early years, and so too, in an analogue, was the early Soviet Union. But over time bureaucracy stifles purposeful action in its central, petty-politics world, and prevents purposeful action in the field, where compliance with central edicts rather than doing the right thing becomes the only imperative. A phrase common in business is that a fish rots from its head down. The first, and

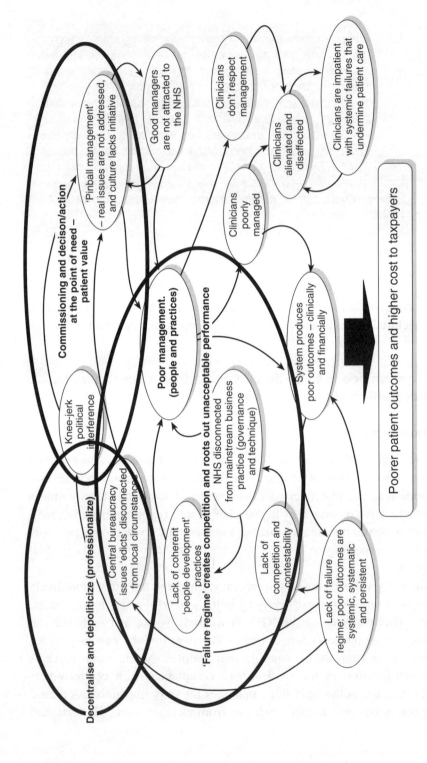

Figure 4.1 Urgent priorities

most effective, step in de-bureaucratizing an organization is to close down as much of the centre as possible – and err on the side of closing down too much rather than too little. The Department of Health (DH) has become a sprawling monster that bureaucratizes much of what it touches. Precise data are not available, but what evidence there is suggests that the DH has grown at an alarming rate.

Of course, detailed 'overhead value analysis' (*not* to be done by expensive consultants) is required to determine exactly what should stay at the centre, what can be pushed out to the regions (the eleven Strategic Health Authorities – SHAs) and what can be cut out entirely. On some estimates, the DH could be reduced to as much as 20 per cent of its current size – and this would increase the productivity of the system by taking out 'make-work' bureaucracy.

The second action that is required is to change the 'quality regime' (which, obviously, in healthcare is particularly important – the definition of 'quality regime' here covers everything from ensuring that doctors and nurses are doing the right things, to ensuring good management practice). In bureaucracies, this is done by defining, in detail, the 'inputs' (the processes that should be followed). This always sounds like a good idea, and it is appropriate in certain service industries – there is, for example, a detailed manual that operatives have to follow to make a McDonald's burger. But in a complex system such as healthcare, where innovation is vital, and where the frontline workers (the doctors and nurses) have to make judgements, then the McDonald's approach is not only wastefully inappropriate (in terms of the time taken to fill in forms) but also dangerous in the way that it (a) diverts doctor and nurse time from the real task at hand – treating patients; but also dangerous in that it (b) makes people feel that they have discharged their duty by adhering to the process rather than judging the specifics of 'this patient in this situation' and using skill and knowledge to do the right thing.

The two contrasting approaches are 'quality inspection' as opposed to 'quality assurance'. The former is the bureaucratic approach and the latter focuses on outcomes, and identifies system failure by (a) creating systems and networks that make best practice available to practitioners, but avoids prescribing mindless adherence to process; and (b) noting statistical variation so that 'failure' can quickly be identified, investigated and corrected. This last point needs to be seen in the context of the comment made earlier in this book – that the IT system being introduced in the NHS has to be made to work (despite the mismanagement of its implementation at the time of writing). It will generate the statistics and data that will allow 'exception reporting'. Good pattern recognition reporting will allow us to forestall tragedies such as the unnecessary infant deaths at Bristol Royal Infirmary, and the long-term killing spree of Dr Harold Shipman.

Michael Porter's book was reviewed extensively in the previous chapter, but he also identifies the failure of the 'quality inspection' regime, and contrasts it with the 'quality assurance' approach:

> Mandatory measurement and reporting of results is perhaps the single most important step in reforming the health care system. Instead of measuring and competing on results, efforts to improve healthcare delivery have made the fundamental error of attempting to control supply and micromanage provider practices ... The whole process-oriented approach is misguided. Standardised process guidelines belie the complexity of individual patient circumstances, and freeze care delivery processes rather than foster innovation ... What is needed is to migrate patients to the truly excellent providers, which feeds a virtuous circle of provider value improvement through greater scale, better efficiency, deeper experience, faster learning, and more dedicated teams and facilities at the medical condition level. In contrast, the lift all boats model perpetuates the vicious circle where many subscale providers lack the capabilities to achieve true excellence. (Porter and Teisberg, *Redefining Healthcare*, p. 7)

Senior managers in the NHS have to drive this culture change through the NHS and all its related organizations. These include, crucially, the Healthcare Commission and Monitor (the body that 'quality assures' Foundation Trusts).

The third thing that needs to happen is to extend the 'quality assurance' process to management practice generally. There is a process-orientated compliance culture also within NHS management. Managers will produce their best results when they are given objectives (which *is* a task that the centre needs to perform), allowed to decide how they are going to meet those objectives without being second-guessed by the bureaucracy, and diverted by the bureaucracy's demands to have all decisions vetted, all plans approved (a process that invariably delays or even cancels decision and change), and all processes inspected. Within the new culture, once the managers have made their decisions and drawn up their plans, they should be left to get on with it. Only when this happens will good management be attracted into the NHS. The next step has to be ruthless – managers who fail to meet their objectives, without any compelling external factors being present, need to be dismissed. They have failed and they need to be replaced by someone who can do better. Failing to be rigorous in rooting out and punishing poor performance also occurs in the private sector, but the necessary actions have to be taken eventually or else the decision is made by customers who put the organization out of business. In the public sector, failure is forgiven and too often covered up – there is no 'customer power' or 'competitive mechanism' to force productive change, and this, together with the civil servants 'looking after their own', means that poor management remains 'trapped' in the NHS. If someone's head does need to roll – often so that politicians can both shift the blame to someone else (and keep their own heads) and 'be seen to be doing something' so that they can avoid ongoing scrutiny – then the taxpayer has to foot an often extravagant redundancy bill.

Modern management practice needs to be introduced urgently into the NHS – and that can only be done by managers who in fact understand modern management practice.

The fourth imperative is to cut out overlapping bureaucracies. The data is available for private hospitals, but it will be similar in the NHS, where forty-eight separate state-directed bodies have the right to make quality inspections. Another 'rule' of bureaucracies is that they tend to proliferate. Not only is there a hugely increased, and distracting, burden on the people who are delivering care, but the internecine strife between these overlapping bureaucracies means that practitioners are pushed around to be compliant with whichever bureaucracy is in the political ascendancy. This proliferation of bureaucratic organizations is abetted by politicians. One of their knee-jerk reactions, outlined in the executive summary, is to respond to the latest crisis by announcing yet another body to oversee or inspect whichever body is currently under attack or out of favour. This type of reaction contributes to the dysfunctional dynamics that is the core diagnosis of this book.

As with the DH, a major culling exercise is required to cut out the superfluous people who work in these overlapping organizations – and no new organization should be introduced unless another is closed down or absorbed into the newcomer.

Decentralize

Closing down large parts of the DH will, of course, result in decentralization as the Regions take on responsibility for achieving defined outcomes. A residual task of the DH would be to agree these outcomes with the SHA chief executives. The chief executives would be responsible for devising plans to achieve the outcomes, and held accountable – with no excuses – for achieving those outcomes. The outcomes would be based on a road map to the vision outlined in the previous chapter. It need be no more complicated than that.

This is different from proposals to create a governance separate from the Department of Health. Former Chancellor Gordon Brown recently talked about this type of approach. Separation of politicians from the running of the NHS, it has been argued in this book, is essential. But it would be of great concern if this proposal meant that central Civil Service management of the NHS was simply replaced by regional Civil Service management. This would not solve any problems – in fact, it would probably make them worse. The only decentralization that makes sense is to put informed choice into the hands of patients and clinicians, and take the civil servants and quangos out of the equation completely – and restrict the politicians to (a) providing very high-level strategic objectives (but even then, only in consultation with clinician experts); and (b) to deciding how much of the taxpayers' money can be spent on the service.

Another worrying interpretation of decentralization is 'democratization'. Again, the worry is that this will translate into onerous governance processes that will be hijacked by local politicians and local civil servants. Real democratization can only be defined in one way – giving the NHS back to the public by creating competition among providers, and letting patients and citizens 'vote' with their feet.

The final point on decentralization is the burning need to re-engage with clinicians. The imperative is to push responsibility out to the front line, and to demand that managers actively manage an environment that provides the most amount of space, choice and discretion for clinicians to work with, and in the best interests of, their patients.

Depoliticize

As the processes of de-bureaucratization and decentralization build momentum they will contribute to achieving the third objective – depoliticization.

Responsibility and accountability must lie with frontline managers and, especially, clinicians. Two further initiatives will also contribute to the objective of depoliticization. The first is the generation of much more data than is currently available within the NHS. The reason mischievous groups – be they the unions or local activists trying to prevent modernization and rationalization of the clinical service – can have such a debilitating impact is that there is little data pointing clearly to the right course of action. The arguments come down to abstract, emotional and uninformed opinions, rather than real hard data. The generation of this data – clinical outcomes and economics – are key themes of this book. The second initiative is to form clinical panels – probably within each SHA – to make clinical judgements on decisions. The evidence that rationalization of services to create units that have greater scale results in greater patient safety is incontrovertible. People might like to keep their 'local hospital' but they need to understand that they are jeopardizing the health and lives of the local people. This evidence has been broadcast by the medical profession for years – from the Chief Medical Officer, Kenneth Calman, thirty years ago, to Bernie Ribeiro, President of the Royal College of Surgeons in recent times. But when local activists try to keep their local hospitals open, the clinicians are not deployed to give their crucial and determinative judgements on what is right from a clinical and safety point of view. We need to deploy these clinicians, armed with the data generated in the first initiative, to break through the uninformed activism and 'democratic' consultation that prevents the eradication of either uneconomic or dangerous situations.

It is sad that NHS management, sixty years on from Bevan, has not solved the problem he identified:

> Bevan had little patience with those who defended small hospitals on grounds of intimacy and local patriotism. 'Although I am not myself a devotee of bigness for bigness sake', he said, 'I would rather be kept alive in the efficient if cold altruism of a large hospital than expire in a gush of warm sympathy in a small one.'[1]

Demand-side mechanisms need to be introduced and extended – patient choice

Patient choice is a crucial ingredient of a reformed, customer-responsive NHS. It is indefensible that even this reform – so central to the idea of a real public service, so crucial as a mechanism for making sure that resources are well-placed and services well-delivered, so morally correct that the patients who, as citizens, pay for the service should have this consumer right – is opposed by many in the NHS. But this opposition does have the perverse logic and rationality that characterizes the dysfunctional NHS and Civil Service. If patients have rights, then they have them at the expense of the providers. If patients exercise choice, then they do so to say that this provider (the monopoly state-run NHS) is inadequate and should be replaced. It quickly becomes very clear that patient choice is a profound threat to a protective and abusive monopoly. The evidence that it is a protective and abusive monopoly *is* that it opposes patient choice.

As was argued earlier – and a core theme of the previous chapter – good information is vital for patients to make informed choices. And the government has scored an own goal by introducing one (choice) without the other, the information on which choice can be based. But once the information deficit is corrected, then patient choice will become an animating mechanism for productive change. The rest of this section looks at the demand for choice across the country.

The latest British Social Attitudes Survey[2] highlights that most people want choice. Contrary to popular prejudice, it also shows that those who are less socially advantaged are more in favour of choice than those who are advantaged. It reveals the falsity of the argument that choice will benefit the middle classes. The reverse is in fact true – in an arcane monopoly NHS, the middle classes are best placed to navigate the system to their advantage. As Julian Le Grand puts it:[3]

> this study also broke down the results by gender, social class and income. And these results many will find quite unexpected.
>
> - 69% of women and 56% of men wanted choice of hospital.
> - 67% of the routine and semi-routine working class wanted choice, compared with 59% of the managerial and professional class.
> - 70% of those earning less than £10,000 p.a. wanted choice, but only 59% of those earning more than £50,000.
> - 69% of those with no educational qualification wanted choice, compared with 56% of those with a higher education qualification.

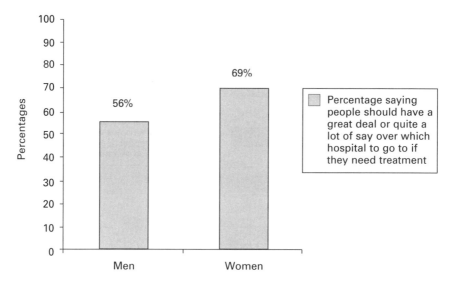

Source: John Appleby and Arturo Alvarez, 'Public Responses to NHS Reform', *British Social Attitudes Survey*, 22nd Report (2005).

Figure 4.2   Who wants choice? Gender

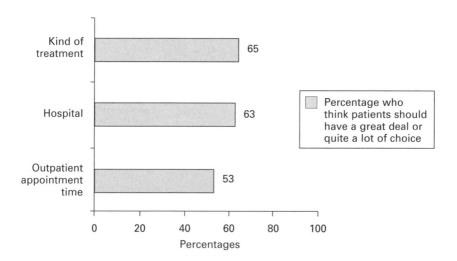

Source: John Appleby and Arturo Alvarez, 'Public Responses to NHS Reform', *British Social Attitudes Survey*, 22nd Report (2005).

Figure 4.3   Should patients have choice?

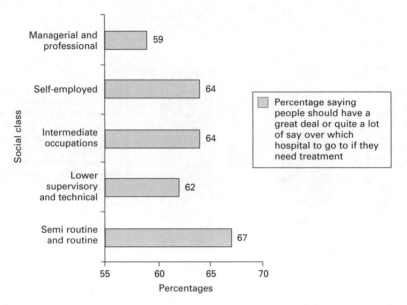

Source: John Appleby and Arturo Alvarez, 'Public Responses to NHS Reform', *British Social Attitudes Survey*, 22nd Report (2005).

Figure 4.4   Who wants choice? Social class

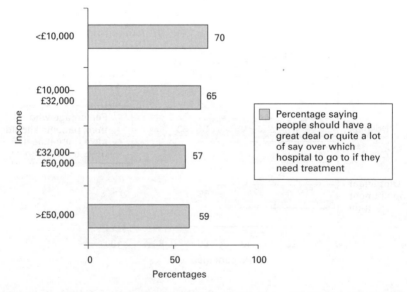

Source: John Appleby and Arturo Alvarez, 'Public Responses to NHS Reform', *British Social Attitudes Survey*, 22nd Report (2005).

Figure 4.5   Who wants choice? Income

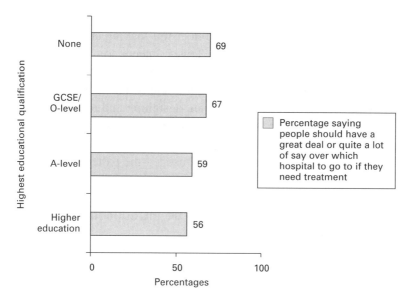

Source: John Appleby and Arturo Alvarez, 'Public Responses to NHS Reform', *British Social Attitudes Survey*, 22nd Report (2005).

Figure 4.6   Who wants choice? Educational qualification

As Le Grand points out succinctly:

Nor, on reflection, should this be surprising. Because it arises from the fact that the middle class already do well out of the unreformed no-choice NHS and education system. With their loud voices, sharp elbows and crucially, their ability to move house if necessary, the middle class get . . . more hospital care relative to need, more preventive care, and better schools . . . In other words, a majority of all groups wanted choice; but it was precisely those groups whom critics of the choice programme think will be disadvantaged by it are the ones who want it most.[4]

Patient choice is the real way that the healthcare system in the UK will be democratized. Well-meaning and principled politicians felt that democratization would best be achieved by creating governance mechanisms within hospitals that would give patients, local constituents, local politicians – anyone in fact – a say in the running of the hospital. This has proved to be a failure; it has resulted in sectional and minority interests usurping patient rights, it has introduced more bureaucracy, and has added to the cacophony that subverts sound decision-making and timely action. This regime – applied to Foundation Trusts – needs to be dismantled. Its introduction in the first place is yet more evidence that the system is being designed and run by (well-meaning) politicians and civil servants who have no knowledge of, or experience in, designing and managing change processes. Their thinking is always 'supply-side' dominated. The only answer is to create demand-side mechanisms that 'pull' reform through – pulled by the demands and rights of the users – the patients.

Demand-side mechanisms need to be introduced and extended – commissioning

A critically important step in dismantling the poorly managed bureaucracy that is the NHS is to separate *commissioning* a service from *providing* a service.

Whether Primary Care Trusts (PCTs) should solely be commissioning bodies, or both commissioners and providers, has become a hot political issue. Following some stiff opposition from professional bodies and trade unions, the government initially backed off from its initial plan to make PCTs commissioning bodies only, and 'clarified' their position by encouraging them to focus on their commissioning role. The idea was that they should sub-contract all their services, including GPs and district nurses. The introduction of this policy was a fiasco. It was announced by NHS Chief Executive Nigel Crisp with little consultation and pre-wiring of people to be affected. Suddenly the revered district nurses, employed currently by the PCTs across the country, did not know who was going to employ them, and whether they would be employed at all. Nothing could be more grist to the Opposition mill than the idea of district nurses being so badly treated – which, of course, they were. Two weeks later, Crisp's deputy, John Bacon, retracted the policy. It sounded as if he was saying 'only joking'. Some say that this is the mismanaged event that cost Sir Nigel Crisp his job. The fact is that the policy was right – but its handling is a poignant example of one of the features of the systemic diagnosis at the core of this book – knee-jerk reactions by politicians ('we haven't announced anything for some time, we need newsflow, let's announce the separation of commissioning and provision') and poor implementation by managers operating in a dysfunctional system.

The issue of commissioning presaged important organizational changes within the NHS, and required a separation of roles at the top of the NHS. The Department of Health restructured its Departmental Board, announcing that:

> NHS chief executive Sir Nigel Crisp's role could be split into two along the same lines, while the NHS top team will be reviewed to see who is fit for the new roles. . . . Consultants from McKinsey have been at Richmond House all week interviewing senior DoH managers.
>
> An insider said: 'It is a no-holds barred look at the top team to see if they are fit for the future. They are looking at radical solutions. Questions should be asked by all parts of the NHS all the time, from the top downwards.' The report is expected early in the New Year and major changes 'are expected'.[5]

The Department of Health[6] finally acknowledged the importance of commissioning and created the new posts of Director of Commissioning and Director of Provider Development. Both Directors will be members of the Departmental Board: 'A number of changes will be made to the Departmental Board. There will be some transitional changes now, and a fully reshaped Board by July.'

Sir Nigel Crisp said in 2005:

> The arrangements we introduced in 2003 put in place a strong delivery and performance management function which means we have been able to help the NHS achieve huge improvements for patients. Now, in order to further lead and shape the reforms, we need to move to a structure that is commissioning-led so that we are equipped to provide strategic leadership for the next set of challenges.

But this is too little too late. The former head of the Department of Health strategy team, Professor Chris Ham, has warned: 'Government health policy has veered into "incoherence" and reforms are dangerously "out of sync" . . . policy has fallen out of sync in the last two years, as too much emphasis has been placed on provision and too little on commissioning.'[7]

This matter was brought to a head by the resignation of Sir Nigel Crisp, and it now appears that his previous post will be split into three:

> The successful candidate may well start out as both permanent secretary of the Department of Health and chief executive of the NHS. But

he or she will be expected to work their way out of the job, which will be split into at least two and probably three separate roles[8] . . . In time, the chief executive role will become that of chief commissioner of NHS services. The permanent secretary's job is likely to be separated out. Another post, as head of NHS provider organisations, is likely to be created to be responsible for the dwindling number of NHS-run organisations. Other NHS bodies will have become foundation trusts or independently contracted organisations run by the staff, with remaining provision coming from the private and voluntary sector.

The government is moving in the right direction, but too cautiously, too slowly and with too little change in senior management. More radical reform is required.

The National Commissioning body should be the group that looks at patient demand and makes national/regional/local allocation decisions on how much should be spent on cancer treatment, for example, as opposed to heart disease, and what should be the most cost-effective spending, whether it be in the primary or secondary care sectors.

Commissioning should be demand-driven and should buy everything from dental services to secondary care within the context of patient choice. Now the NHS too often starts from the supply side, where innovations are adapted to fit the bureaucracy instead of supply being evolved to fit demand/need.

There is also a need for competent regional commissioning bodies that plan regional health needs from the demand perspective – from the point of view of patient need. This could be achieved by merging all current public-sector competing and overlapping bodies (PCTs and Care Trusts) into around 120 regional commissioning bodies.

The commissioning process is analogous to a linear program where the objective function is defined (for example, to extend life expectancy) against various boundary constraints (for example, available resources and demographics).

More specifically commissioning is the process of:

- *Determining the health needs of a region.* Healthcare needs in heavily populated and inner-city areas are likely to be very different from those in suburban and rural areas. Although there will always be national healthcare objectives, one size never fits all, and each region will need to fine tune its priorities according to its own identified needs, which will be determined by a variety of factors – social class, poverty, age profile, ethnicity and so on. This would entail building an epidemiology map for each region. Such data exists in some cases – but it is incomplete, inconsistent and not widely distributed.

- *Designing and adopting care pathways* for these conditions and introducing, where appropriate, chronic disease management. As Michael Porter's new research in the USA shows, continuity of care over the disease/treatment cycle will produce better health outcomes. This perspective from the patient's point of view – instead of the supply-side point of view – will radically change the way our healthcare system is designed. In particular, it will break down the ridiculous divide between primary and secondary care, which in the UK institutionalizes fragmented patient care.

- *Combining the epidemiology map with the care pathways* to produce a 'Better Health Outcomes Model' that describes how the specific health needs of a region can be met and outcomes improved.

- *Defining the objective of the regional healthcare economy* and allocating scarce resources against explicit trade-offs, so that the optimal solution is reached. The first task is to define the 'objective function', draw the boundary constraints, such as resources, and identify the optimal solution. Once an integrated pathway for diabetes is developed, for example, then an area with a high incidence of diabetes (which occurs, for instance, in areas where a high proportion of the population is Asian) the decision would probably be made to put more of the regional budget into managing this disease than might be the case in an area with a lower incidence. It would, of course, influence the whole design of the healthcare infrastructure.

- *Commissioning the best provider*, public, private or voluntary sector to deliver the solution. The issue is not, and never should have been, public versus private, but rather which provider can best serve British patients at the lowest cost to British taxpayers. Gordon Brown's recent opinion that there are 'limits to privatization' misses the point. It is an opinion that profoundly betrays the public-sector perspective, rather than the citizens.' The only determinant of how much of the provider base is private, public or voluntary should be which organization can do the best job, defined by the patient's choice to use it.

• *Performance managing the provider*, and if necessary replacing poor performers. As part of this process, collect the data that will allow reassessment and refinement of the 'Better Health Outcomes Model'. The commissioner defines the market context within which patients can exercise choice or, in the case of a 'natural monopoly', the commissioner will become the customer who, based on clinical outcome data, decides which organization gets the right to serve patients.

This whole commissioning process is a never-ending cycle. Commissioning is, in effect, the 'keeper' of the public good:

• Making optimal allocation decisions; and
• Making sure that the taxpayers' money is spent appropriately.

The virtuous circle is shown in Figure 4.7.

The commissioning function should not be confused with the provision of care. The separation is essential in creating an improved healthcare service for UK citizens. In the first place, our system has suffered from not having a commissioning function across three areas:

• We have developed no epidemiological expertise in the field. Our allocation of taxpayers' money is not directed at clear objectives with clear trade-offs. We do not know if we are spending the right relative amounts of money on, say, cancer compared to heart disease.
• We have failed to integrate care pathways from a patient's point of view – the most significant being the poor integration between primary and secondary care.
• There has been no 'voice of the customer'. This has engendered a supply side/provider's emphasis, and the patient has not been at

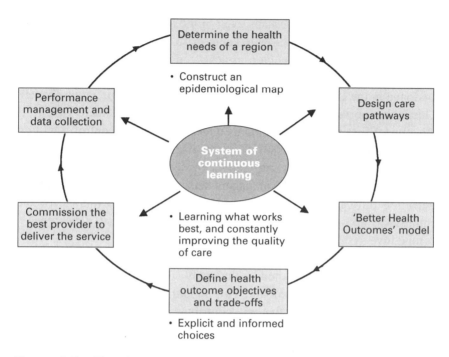

Figure 4.7 The virtuous circle of commissioning

the centre of the system. An example of this emphasis was demonstrated recently when a survey of patients in the NHS came up with a number of complaints (and compliments). The reaction of the NHS audience who received this feedback was that people should not criticize the NHS because 'it's bad for the morale of NHS employees, and, after all, we are a public sector organization'. This is, of course, back to front. The customers are the patients, not the NHS. Customer feedback is essential for any organization if it is interested in improving performance.

As long as commissioning and providing stay together, then not only will we not solve the three problems detailed above, but the commissioners will commission themselves also to be the providers. Monopolies, in the private or public sectors, inevitably make decisions that will defend themselves. Therefore, competition and best practice, delivered by the best provider, will be stillborn.

In the short term, and perhaps even in the medium term, commissioning should be run as a state-owned enterprise. But the logic of the vision outlined in the previous chapter argues strongly that the commissioning role needs to be opened up to competition. Commissioning has its analogue in the USA in health plans, as discussed in the previous chapter. This is the 'portal' through which patients enter the healthcare system. If this crucial first port of call remains under government control it will go the same way as the bigger NHS system itself – it will open with initial enthusiasm, but then drift into self-interested, unionized usurpation of citizens' rights. Senior NHS managers need to get this right – we need a transition through the state monopoly phase (taking advantage of the enthusiasm and good intent), but also to make sure that it becomes a competitive system in the not-too-distant future.

Once this happens, we need to have in place a body that makes sure the commissioners are monitored – that public money is well spent and patients' interests are paramount. This should not require the creation of yet another statutory body that will contribute to the bureaucratic cacophony. What is needed is a staged, well-managed transition of the current SHA chief executives to this role as guardians of the public purse. They will be the 'visible hand' that keeps the healthcare economy above board.

Demand-side mechanisms need to be introduced and extended – primary care

Primary care is in dire need of reform. The old family GP model worked well in the period after 1948, but is no longer appropriate for the modern world. At a more fundamental level, the old GP model is failing the poorest members of society. This is another example of where the NHS has actually increased health inequality. Poor districts such as Tower Hamlets have far below the average number of GPs per capita, and a lower spend compared to middle-class areas. There is strong evidence that the old system of GPs exacerbates health inequalities and needs to be changed.[9]

In the twenty-first century, citizens need greater and more flexible access, preferably over 24 hours a day, seven days a week. A telephone service and website-based information is a start, but is no substitute for primary care embedded in the local community. There is a need for more services at the primary care level, such as on-site imaging and diagnostics as well as minor injuries treatment, integrated professional healthcare communities and a wider choice of providers.

Choice of providers is an important issue, for three material reasons. As Paul Corrigan[10] puts it:

1. Primary care is the main experience that the public has of the National Health Service . . . since one of the main aims of reform is to systematically empower the public and patient, a failure to approach patient centred reform in primary care would lead to a failure of reform as a whole.
2. Primary care in all its manifestations will continue to act not just as the main provider of health services but as the gatekeeper to all other services. If patients do not feel that their primary care empowers them, then they will feel disempowered in this crucial gate keeping relationship.
3. The primary care relationship is much more constant than that of secondary care, which is mainly episodic in nature. Thus, the argument for patient empowerment in a continuing relationship with a GP is much more powerful in terms of developing individuals' ability to effect their own health programme.

He goes on to say:

Increasing capacity in primary care will not only make choice of GP a reality for a larger number of people, but will also provide the possibility of offering very clear alternatives with diverse mechanisms of supply to choose between. That means not only having different models of supply, but also different forms of delivery.

One benefit of the commissioning process that is being advocated here is that it will integrate a system that has become fragmented between primary care (GPs) and secondary care (acute hospitals). This fragmentation prevents the development of integrated care pathways. In orthopaedics, for example, this would entail new pre-operative assessment processes including rehabilitation advice and liaison with community equipment services followed by use of step-down intermediate care services to support direct discharge to the patient's home.

Most people today do not understand the artificial separation between health and social care. Although full integration may be difficult as these two services have different cultures and should meet different, but linked, demands and needs (but there is so much defensiveness on both sides that this piece of 'conventional wisdom' could well do with some serious challenge), they can be integrated at the commissioning stage. Regional commissioning bodies can commission to both sides, health services and social services, and in some cases – for example, chronic disease management in the aged – develop an integrated solution. This would be done through integrated 'case management' so that one person has a 'prime contractor' role in navigating the patient through the system. This type of integrated case management will have a powerful impact on improving the lot of the most disadvantaged in our society.

Changing citizen needs suggest that the traditional GP model should be replaced by a more modern style of organization. This organization would be based on a 'company' model, in which GPs and other healthcare professionals are employed on a salary or equity basis (in the case of a 'for-profit' organization) or as a social-equity partner in a 'not-for-profit' organization. Only this type of model can deliver a mechanism that is responsive to population needs, allocates investment resources against those needs, and deploys the essential, sophisticated management talent.

There has been some research done on what patients want, as part of the production of the 2005 White Paper on Primary Healthcare. The data below is taken from the consultation exercise in Leicester.

Major issues identified by Leicester consumer/citizen group (multiple choice answers receiving the highest percentage agreement)

QUESTION ONE: HOW CAN PEOPLE LOOK AFTER THEMSELVES? HOW CAN WE HELP YOU TAKE CARE OF YOURSELF AND SUPPORT YOU AND YOUR FAMILY IN YOUR DAILY LIVES?
1d: Ensuring older people and those with disabilities can get the practical help and support they need to remain independent and active for longer – 33 per cent.
1a: Encouraging and supporting better health; for example, through routine check-ups, advice on healthy lifestyles and promoting self-care and self-assessment – 32 per cent.

QUESTION TWO: HOW CAN WE HELP YOU GET THE RIGHT
SERVICES AND MAKE SURE YOUR CARE AND SUPPORT IS
PROPERLY JOINED UP?

2a: Providing effectively joined-up social care and health services to
those that need them; for example, through a single 'needs assessment'
and use of case managers. A 'needs assessment' would be a kind of
one-stop-shop appointment instead of many different appointments, a
case manager would be someone who plans care with the patient and
then co-ordinates it – 27 per cent.

2b: Providing more help to people caring for others; for example, with
more respite care – 27 per cent.

QUESTION THREE: WHEN YOU AND YOUR FAMILY NEED
HELP AND SUPPORT, HOW, WHEN, WHERE AND FROM
WHOM DO YOU WANT TO GET IT?

3c: Developing and providing more services in the local community,
rather than only in hospitals, so they are more convenient for people to
use. For example, blood tests, X-rays, some scans, minor surgery and
physiotherapy could be provided locally. Also, hospital specialists
could run clinics in the community – 33 per cent.

3a: Providing convenient services that fit around people's lives; for
example, by extending opening hours to evenings and weekends at the
local GP practice, pharmacy and other community services – 25 per
cent.

From this NHS research, it is clear that there are five ways in which the
existing model of organization of GP services needs to be improved:

1. *People want more health advice.* They want a health service and
   not just a sickness service. GPs must have the knowledge to
   further the public health agenda with advice on lifestyle changes
   including advice on a healthy diet, reducing the amount of
   unsafe sex, how to stop smoking and so on. This would also
   address the evolving role of the GP, which is shifting from
   absolute authority figure to facilitator of patient-led healthcare.
2. *People want out-of-hours access to GPs.* The restrictions that
   limit GPs working out of hours have to be repealed. Setting up
   Health Centres that will create the economies of scale required to

manage a service that is open for more hours will facilitate this. In order to release the hours for GPs to spend more time giving health advice, their workflow can be redesigned, placing more front-line work with nurses. There needs to be regular customer feedback and a central role for professional management.

3. *People want to receive more services*, such as routine X-rays, scans, minor procedures and other investigative/diagnostic procedures in the local community. The need is for more elaborate Health Centres, each accommodating at least ten GPs. These Centres would have scanning equipment and basic pathology units. A minor injuries service should be offered, as this would increase people's awareness of the services available. With the extra equipment, there would be more opportunity to provide screening services.

4. *Citizens want a more 'joined up' service in terms of social care* on the one hand, and healthcare on the other. People are puzzled by the different regimes that rule social care (largely via the Local Authority) and healthcare (mainly the NHS), and they are bewildered by the need for multiple appointments and the often-inefficient duplication of roles. These distinctions need to be eliminated. The separation of social care and healthcare resulted from a struggle in 1948 between Aneurin Bevan and Ernest Bevin. The latter wanted to keep power with the local authorities, rather than surrender it to central government. Bevan and Bevin could not find common ground, so Bevan took healthcare responsibilities away from local authorities, and, famously, created the National Health Service. The centre of gravity of social care remained at the local level. This arcane, long-forgotten political tussle is irrelevant to citizens in the twenty-first century. The key is to create a commissioning body that encompasses both social and healthcare: a body that integrates the two services.

5. *Older people want to be helped to remain active*. The current structure encourages older citizens to become dependent on home-delivered services, but does little to encourage the moderately infirm senior citizen to get out and about, exercise and socialize. In a population where the number and proportion of seniors is steadily increasing, initiatives to encourage senior activity and health will be ever more important.

There are two further things that have to happen in order for the five reforms listed above to work:

1. *The creation of larger Health Centres.* These will give the economies of scale and scope required to:

   • Organize the critical mass of GPs (at least ten per centre) that will allow for rotas, which in turn will allow near-24-hour operation.
   • Consolidate the demand to justify a greater mass of equipment (including MRI/CT scanning in major centres) and services. The importance of moving diagnostics out of hospitals and into Health Centres was highlighted by the *Financial Times* analysis of Department of Health data: 'And while extra MRI scans and other forms of diagnostics are being installed in the NHS and bought from the private sector, health economists say there is good international evidence that the first effect of that may well be a rise in demand as patients who would not now be sent (to hospital) for a scan because the wait is so long to become eligible for one.[11]

   The advantages of scale are illustrated in Figure 4.8.

2. GP practices need to have more *professional management* (the major theme, of course, of this book) that can act on customer needs, and design efficient work practices. An important function of better management will be to market services better. Some misunderstanding surrounds the words 'consumerism' and 'marketing' in the public sector: 'Consumerism' is not some sort of mechanical, and rather shady, practice; and marketing does *not* mean advertising. These words, in reality, describe processes that:

   • Seek to understand what customers want and need;
   • Design services that meet those wants and needs; and
   • Seek to provide information that allows consumers to access those services.

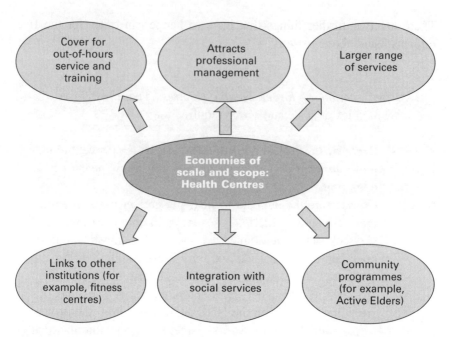

Figure 4.8 Health Centres are at the core of the recommended reforms in primary care

The third function is particularly important in designing a consumer- and citizen-led health service. Lack of information is a major complaint currently – and probably an important driver of health inequalities in that the 'better off', as was argued earlier, seek, find and use information better than those who are worse off. Designing information in ways that are accessible to, and usable by, consumers (instead of being a dump of 'public information') is a vital part of good management. Finally, the function of professional management will be to manage efficiency, so that more services can be offered to the public at a lower cost to the taxpayer. As part of the introduction of professional management into the Health Centres, all other bureaucratic organizations/institutions that currently exist should be closed down or, at the very least, cut to a minimum, and all managerial/admin resources should be placed as close as possible to the point where services are delivered to citizens.

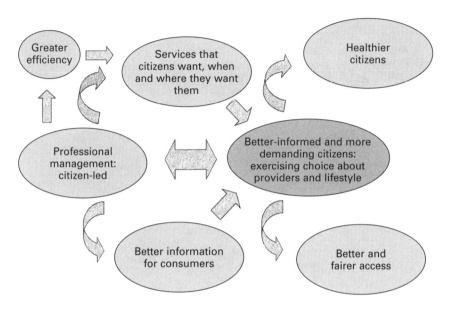

Figure 4.9   'Consumerism'

This issue of 'consumerism' having nasty connotation in the mouths of public service employees is important. In the sense of it putting patients at the centre of the NHS (and citizens, more broadly, at the centre of public service), it *is* the mindset change that needs to occur.

Figures 4.9 and 4.10 illustrate what consumerism means, and why the alternative (the Civil Service monopoly) is, from a citizen's point of view, an unacceptable alternative.

The number of patients being treated in hospitals, resulting in additional cost to the NHS, when their condition could and should be managed at the primary care level, further illustrates a real need for radical reform of primary care:

The ageing of the population will mean an increase in the number of people with long-term conditions, such as chronic lung disease, heart disease and diabetes. Already, more than 15 million people live with these conditions, accounting for half of GP consultations and 75% of time spent in a hospital bed ... However, many of these emergency admissions could be avoided and people supported to manage their

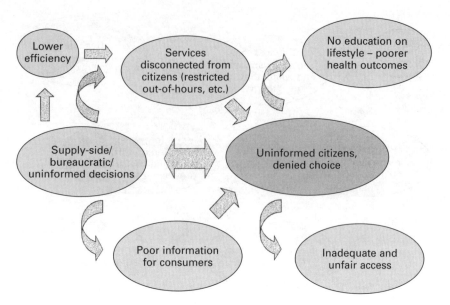

Figure 4.10   The unacceptable alternative

condition through the right combination of health and social care, as long as care is provided at the right time. By focusing on these people, there is an opportunity for the NHS to improve their quality of life and to do so in a way that makes better use of scarce health resources. This is an immediate and achievable challenge, with £2.3 billion of NHS money at stake.[12]

The issue of better marketing underscores the importance of patients having access to better information than is now currently available. A 'one size fits all' approach to public services clearly fails to understand diversity in our society and this failure leads, in turn, to an information base that is not only inaccessible, but also excludes many citizens from the kind of information they need.

A MORI poll based on a survey of 1,276 people aged 40-plus and carried out between 20 and 24 January 2005 illustrated the paucity of healthcare information. When asked the question 'The government is developing a new policy to offer people using the NHS more choice about their treatment. How much, if anything, have you heard about this new initiative?', the results were as shown here:

	Percentage
A great deal	4
A fair amount	15
Just a little	39
Nothing at all	41
Don't know	1

Source: *Patient Choice*, 'Final Topline Results',
1 February 2005.

More recently, the *British Medical Journal*, drawing on a St James's University Hospital survey of over 125 primary care trusts, concluded that: 'Patient choice is being undermined by poor monitoring of the quality of care being provided.'[13] Researchers found that the methods used to monitor care varied from area to area in the survey. Report author Dr Paul Brogden (using the example of cataract care) concluded:

> The public expect that safe cataract care should be commissioned for them and robust methods of monitoring need to be agreed and implemented so that patients can make a truly informed choice. These decisions need to be made not only for cataract surgery but also for other elective procedures that will increasingly be made available to patients through the patient choice scheme.[14]

The government has made a start in addressing the lack of healthcare information by setting up a joint venture between the Health and Social Care Information Centre (HSCIC) and Dr Foster Holdings LLP (Dr Foster Intelligence). The aim of the new company is:

> To improve use and accessibility of information across the health and care system, in support of the overall aim of giving people more choice and control over health and social care. It will compete with other providers of management information solutions to support better commissioning, choice, quality and efficiency: all areas of the reform programme where better use of information by patients, users, professionals and managers is vital.[15]

So, what kind of information do people need?

First, they need to know *when GP practices are open and what kinds of services they provide*. They also need to know whether the GP practice has space on its register for a new person. At present, most practices have similar opening times and existing information on PCT leaflets and websites is therefore not a lever for making choices.

Second, they need to know about the *specific services and treatments that a GP practice offers and to have access to data about health outputs and outcomes*. At the time of writing, there is very little information available about GP practices because of the odd situation that the Healthcare Commission cannot inspect GP practices because they are not 'NHS organizations'. This situation needs to change, and the Healthcare Commission should be given powers to inspect GP practices.

Third, people need *qualitative information*. A patient, for example, who has diabetes, is far more likely to learn how to manage his or her condition from someone else who has diabetes than from a doctor. The NHS Expert Patient programme has been a success for that reason and should be expanded. Expert Patients can give a person who is about to register with a GP the kind of qualitative information they want and need. A good GP marketing strategy would entail the utilization of Expert Patients.

This raises the question of who is going to provide this information. At present PCTs have a duty to provide information about primary care in their area. But, that requirement is very limited in its scope and does not differentiate between the different providers. Paul Corrigan is right in saying that there is a need for the public and private sector to work jointly in providing information:

> We need to blend two very different approaches to answering the question of who is going to provide healthcare information. The public sector approach to providing information would be to set up a public organisation as a source of reliable information, and state that if information comes from this source it can be trusted – but if it comes from anywhere else, you are on your own . . . The alternative private sector model would be to turn this information into a commodity. Recognising that this commodity has a price for consumers, and believing that somewhere somebody will buy the commodity, will make the generation of information financially viable. Quality will be controlled by competition between providers and by consumers who will decide that firm x produces good quality data whilst firm y does not. It would be useful of course to blend these drivers for information and improvement . . . So both drivers for providing information – the public and the private sector – will continue and a partnership between the two is

likely to establish greater strength than competition. The NHS needs the entrepreneurial activity of private enterprises that ensure that their product is timely and of relevance to the people that need it. And the entrepreneur needs the NHS and government to ensure that the information is collected and generated correctly and reliably. This is the field that could be best served by a joint venture, requiring greater co-ordination between these two sectors.[16]

Clearly, there is a need for the Healthcare Commission to collect and make available reliable and appropriate GP data. The private healthcare sector could play an invaluable role in the dissemination of that data. As Paul Corrigan puts it:

> The Government must acknowledge the value of private sector informatics providers as an effective means of disseminating information to a wider audience than any single state provider will be able to reach. Consequently, it is the responsibility of Government to ensure the same transparent and efficient performance monitoring is carried out in primary care as in secondary care and that this information is held in the public realm to allow the market for information to grow and new providers to establish themselves.

This reform should be implemented sooner rather than later, if 'patient choice' is going to be meaningful and effective.

Finally, the issue of the GP's skill set needs to be debated and refined, through discussion of what works, over the next few years. There is clearly a need for the GP/counsellor role. The traditional 'Dr Finlay' model needs, however, to be supplemented by the counsellor being much better skilled in integrating health and social care: many GPs need to become the frontline in this health and social care integration. This is a bigger challenge than it might seem, as not only are two separate systems operating at the time of writing, but the practitioners in each are suspicious of each other and sometimes hostile. Within the GP community there will probably be a need for functions to be differentiated, probably involving GPs with different 'majors', in the sense of being specially trained – or even dedicated – to a single function. Specifically, better diagnostic skills are needed in GPs, and this would probably require them to specialize in, say, obstetrics, or respiratory disease, or diabetes and so on. This specialization will make the logic for larger, scale-efficient health centres even stronger, so that there is at least one specialist based at each centre. One of these specialities is, as the government has identified, a minor surgery capability.

Over time, as the GP service professionalizes, we shall begin to see more 'catalogues of services', to enable patients to know what is available to them. Given the almost unlimited demand for healthcare and, of course, limited money to pay for it, there will be a need to be much more explicit about what treatments and facilities patients can access via the NHS and what they cannot. This will put an end to many of the distracting headlines about, for example, whether scarce NHS money should be spent on free parking!

Competition needs to be introduced

One of the important reforms that the government has introduced in the last couple of years has been the introduction of (very limited) competition by inviting the private sector to deliver some elective surgery to NHS patients.

This needs to be put into context. In the first place, the private sector has been providing capacity to the NHS for many years. At times, especially since waiting list targets were introduced in the NHS, as many as 150,000 patients per annum could receive treatment in the private sector. These procedures were generally charged at private-sector rates for a private-sector service:

- A single room with much greater privacy and dignity, hotel-compatible service, much greater nurse attention (that is, more nurses per patient).
- Much more individualized attention from the consultant (the private sector creates an environment which is higher quality – in terms of patient outcomes – but requires skilled consultants and their clinical team to spend much less time on meaningless bureaucracy).
- A much better-managed environment which centres on the patient and the skill of the doctor. The doctors are supported in doing what they are trained to do – look after their patients.
- Treatment by highly experienced consultants and not by their 'learner' subordinates.

This sounds like a plug for private healthcare – and it is. Almost 50 per cent of NHS consultants themselves have private health insurance. But in fact, the truth is different. NHS patients are much easier to acquire by private healthcare companies than private patients – there is no marketing required as they are directed to the hospital after an agreement is reached with the PCT or acute trust. They can be scheduled into theatre slots as and when is convenient to the hospital (unlike private patients, who, quite rightly, want to be treated when it is convenient to *them*). The fixed costs of the private hospitals are there in any case, and this is the crucial point, so any NHS volume provides full revenue for little extra cost (on the whole). So even if NHS volumes are only 3 per cent or 4 per cent of private hospital revenue, they make a large contribution to profit. The fact that private hospitals were being paid full private-sector rates for NHS patients was another example of NHS naivety and inefficiency. What is more, the purchases by the NHS were 'distress purchases'. At the end of the NHS's financial year (end of April) they would realize they were going to breach their waiting list targets and would pay to meet them (as missing them would result in a reprimand), so public money was used to solve their problem.

This is one of the difficulties that Ken Anderson, an American with private-sector experience, was faced with when he took on the job of commercial director for the NHS some years ago. Anderson realized that if he centralized and tendered for private-sector companies to build new hospital capacity and committed contractually to treating specified numbers of NHS patients at a tendered (and, therefore, low) price, he could hugely reduce the taxpayers' burden. He also realized that there was very little competition within the private sector.

So, as director of the NHS Commercial Directorate, he embarked on a procurement process. He brought real drive and strategic vision to the project. Very significantly, these characteristics were in deep contrast to those of his Civil Service colleagues. The results were stunning. Private-sector rates charged to the NHS halved. New private-sector (but NHS-dedicated) hospitals were planned – called Independent Sector Treatment Centres (ISTCs). But the most extraordinary effect of this competitive threat (and to be clear, this was not a current reality, but rather a future threat) was that it combined with the government's targeting of patient waiting lists to spur action in the NHS. Two types of action were taken. As mentioned earlier in this book, one action that Trust CEOs took was to try to pre-empt the possible future arrival of private competition by building capacity in their region so they could claim that there was sufficient capacity there, and therefore no need to build an ISTC. We now have a situation of excess capacity in a number of places – empty wards at the taxpayers' expense. The second type of action was more productive, as Trusts began to organize themselves a bit better. As they trawled through the lists, they discovered that much of the data they had was poor – some patients that were on the list had, in fact, died while waiting for treatment. And for those patients still needing treatment, the Trusts worked hard to have them treated within the target set by the government – in many cases, as in the past, using the private sector to clear their lists. The result was that the Labour government achieved a considerable success:

> The Labour party's 1997 election manifesto promised to reduce the numbers of patients waiting for hospital treatment after an initial appointment with a consultant – inpatients list – by 100,000. This target was achieved in 2000. Numbers have been falling ever since, and now stand at 843,923.[17]

> Labour has succeeded in eliminating the longest waiting times for hospital treatment. By November 2004, no one was waiting more than 18 months, and only 140 people were waiting over 12 months. Just under 62,000 people were waiting more than six months – a figure the government is confident it can eliminate, having cut the total by more than this number in the previous year . . . Now, no one waits more than six months for an operation, but by 2008 we'll have cut that to a maximum of 18 weeks for the entire patient journey from GP referral to treatment, and where the average time will be just four weeks.[18]

> The contribution of the independent sector was summarized as follows:

> - Over 250,000 patients have been either treated by or received a diagnostic service from the independent sector
> - Patient satisfaction is running at over 94%
> - In 2006, ISTCs are expected to treat a further 145,000 NHS patients
> - 'Value for money has been achieved by cutting what the NHS used to spend'[19]

This small injection of private-sector competition had a disproportionate effect in bringing down waiting lists. It also delivered productivity and efficiency gains that provide a new benchmark for the NHS. The productivity and efficiency gains independent treatment centres have pioneered are outlined by the Department of Health as follows:

- Mobile units capable of delivering up to 20–23 ophthalmology cases per day due to streamlined procedures enabling efficient use of theatre space and surgical resource
- Administering local instead of general anaesthetic for some joint replacements, reducing the anaesthetic risk as well as the period of stay by the patient to an average of 5.3 days from 8 days in the NHS
- Introducing blood conservancy and recycling techniques that reduce the need for transfusions
- Using effective pain management techniques to allow post-operative physiotherapy to commence earlier thus reducing the length of stay[20]

Other benefits, according to the Department of Health, that ISTCs have brought to the NHS include: 'faster treatment', 'more capacity' and 'greater choice'.

The waiting list improvements were achieved with little, if any, new private-sector capacity coming on stream – merely the threat of it (and targets) was enough to force action. The ISTC programme, in that sense, has been a success. But it has also failed in a couple of respects. The bureaucracy of the NHS, together with quite a bit of 'spoiling' by local Trusts faced with a local ISTC project, has meant that the programme has taken far longer to implement than it should.

More importantly, the tiny amount of competition the private-sector ISTCs bring is not going to affect the vast bulk of the NHS. The private sector is unlikely to represent more than around 5 per cent p.a. of the NHS spend over the next decade or so. This is not going to create real competition. The ISTC programme was launched on the assumption that there was a shortage of beds and operating theatres. However, this was not case – the real shortage was, and remains, a competent management that can use the facilities wisely. But the ISTC programme was, more importantly, a political own-goal. It is useful, but not essential, in the process of creating competition. Much more powerful is to challenge the core clinical units within the NHS to become competitive – for the clinically successful units, the more ambitious units and the more patient-orientated units to take over the failing clinical units elsewhere in the system. The government could have introduced competition on the back of favourable news reports about effective NHS units taking over ineffective ones. Instead, its reforms are constantly undermined by 'privatization' taunts.

The lack of real competition introduced by the private sector is a problem, given the central importance of competition in driving the healthcare economy down the road to being patient-centred. The answer is to create competition within the NHS. The Foundation Trusts need to be given unfettered rights to become national players. They should be actively encouraged to compete to provide clinical services anywhere in the country. An immediate step would be to identify ten or so clinical units that are failing around the country – there are many of them, and they are well known – and put them out to tender to Foundation Trusts. This would be the first step in a programme that, through commissioners, creates a market in all parts of the country.

There would be two types of competition within the British healthcare economy:

- Competition that gives patients continuous and real choice, as in the case of competing GP practices; and
- Competition that gives patients choice of which management team or organization should operate a 'natural monopoly' over a period of time. For example, it would be difficult, in the medium term, to justify competing A&E departments because of insufficient scale, confusion for patients and no opportunity to exercise real choice. The 'natural monopoly' would operate against strict performance criteria, and the contract would be up for competitive tender after a predetermined (say, 5 years) period. Of course, if the commissioners had information that units were underperforming, then the contract would be terminated and a new, and better, provider (a Foundation Trust team from elsewhere) would step in.

The only criterion for who provides the healthcare service is who produces the best health outcomes at the lowest cost to UK taxpayers. Patient choice not only returns the NHS to one of Bevan's founding principles, but it also tackles health inequalities.

It is interesting how healthcare is put, inappropriately, into a separate category from consumers' daily experiences. Most people would realize, for example, that if one supermarket giant was granted a monopoly on groceries, over time the company would inevitably abuse their position, and that customer service, choice and prices would suffer. Yet the obvious extension of this truism to healthcare is a mental leap – but it is a leap that has to be made if the citizens are going to take back control of their rights.

A strong argument for the importance of competition, and what is required to make it happen, was made in a King's Fund report produced in June 2006. The summary recommendations of that report are shown below.[21] The summary recommendations are repeated verbatim. The author of this book was a participant in the King's Fund Report, so it might not be surprising that most of its recommendations echo the views expressed in this book. But two things are important to note. First, the author of this book disagrees with only three of the thirty-four recommendations in the King's Fund report – and even then, only mildly. But, second and much more importantly, the majority of the working group that produced the King's Fund Recommendations were NHS managers. Of course, they were selected because they are open-minded, but it is also encouraging that there are some people in the NHS who understand the need for change, and the direction in which it needs to go. One general error the report makes is not to focus enough on the demand side, and in particular on the importance of published data on patient outcomes. However, given the almost complete absence of this perspective in the UK healthcare system of the past forty or so years, this is understandable.

The King's Fund commissioned an independent working party to explore how the supplier market could work in health care. This group, chaired by Greg Parston, made a number of recommendations

1. The government needs to state unequivocally that it sees a supplier market in healthcare as the long-term future for the national health system. It should not, as ministers have tended to do so far, state or imply an upper limit to independent sector provision. The proportion of care coming from NHS-run, private and voluntary sectors should emerge from the operation of the market. It should not be artificially defined.

2. Ministers need to understand that in future they will be responsible for a national health system, not a state-owned national health service. Their role will be to raise the money for the NHS from the Treasury, define broad priorities and set the regulatory framework. But

they will not then be involved in the day-to-day management of the service. Instead a commissioner will buy it from whoever offers the best value and quality.

3. Ministers need to explain this clearly not only to the public but to their own backbenchers and other members of parliament. As that happens, MPs, councillors and others will need to understand that their role is to defend the quality of services to patients, not institutions.

4. Primary care trusts' future role will primarily be commissioning, co-ordination, and an element of regulation, not direct provision of services. They will primarily be responsible for the purchase of care for patients – charged with ensuring that care is there, not that particular institutions, whether run by the NHS or not, thrive or survive.

5. Even as they seek to make the NHS more responsive, and to increase choice, politicians also need to be honest with the public in explaining that in any collectively funded system of health care, there will be limits to choice

6. In the short to medium term (short defined as six months, medium as perhaps two to four years) there is a case for retaining a joint post of permanent secretary/chief executive of the NHS. In the medium term, however, its functions must be separated. Whoever takes the post needs to understand that their job is to work their way out of it, creating one of the two following structures.

Either:

- A policy arm headed by ministers and a permanent secretary, responsible for raising cash for the NHS from the Treasury, setting broad policy goals and the regulatory framework.
- A commissioner of NHS services, operating as a separate entity at arms length from the Department of Health and using that budget to buy care for patients.
- A separate head of NHS operations, again a statutorily distinct entity from the Department of Health, responsible for NHS-run organisations – a role that will diminish over time as more hospitals and other services acquire foundation trust status, and as more primary care and community staff leave formal NHS employment to form their own businesses to supply the NHS.

Or:

- A combined post of permanent secretary/chief executive of the NHS with remaining NHS-run organisations hived off into a statutorily separate NHS Provider organisation whose role will diminish, probably to the point of extinction.

On the balance of the current debate, the majority of the working group favoured the first of these two options.

7. To speed and ease this transformation, NHS trusts need to move as rapidly as possible to the foundation trust financial regime: handling cash budgets as businesses and able to borrow to invest. Initially, because of their legal status, this borrowing will have to come from an NHS bank. The current NHS accounting system, with its statutory duty to break even on a given day, must go and be replaced by one that reflects a trust's position as a going concern.

8. The government was right in its July 2005 circular to argue that primary care trusts should primarily become commissioners not providers. It was wrong in the way it handled it. This split needs to be made, but it needs to evolve, not be enforced everywhere overnight.

9. When NHS staff form new not-for-profit businesses to supply NHS care, for contracts of any size above, say, a few million pounds a year, the service should as a matter of good practice be offered for tender, even though this is not a legal requirement. Where it is judged that for the time being it is more important to hive off the service, to create a broad purchaser/provider split within PCTs rather than to ensure full competition, such contracts should, as a matter of principle, be put out to tender on renewal. The NHS has done this before when, for example, the then regional health authorities got rid of their architects' departments in the 1990s.

10. The government must explore in more detail and reach decisions on regulation. The working group's view is that to attempt a merger now between the Commission for Social Care Inspection and the Healthcare Commission is not advisable. At present the very different nature of their markets, eligibility rules and payment mechanisms militate against that. It is an issue that should be left for another day, although joint working between the two needs to be strengthened.

11. Monitor's role will clearly expand as more NHS organisations gain foundation trust status. Its key task is to oversee the financial viability of foundation trusts, while having powers to require them to provide services if a PCT so insists. Its current role does not embrace competition issues, and it would face a conflict of interest were that to be added.

12. The working group's tentative view is that the quality inspector – the Healthcare Commission – should remain a separate body, reporting on standards and quality. It should increasingly focus on the quality of commissioning.

13. The setting of the tariff should be moved out of the Department of Health to an independent body, working to published guidelines set by ministers.

14. There is a need for a competition regulator, dealing with issues of local monopoly referred to it either by other providers, or by commissioners who find their normal purchasing powers cannot break a local monopoly that they no longer judge to be in patients' interests.

15. This body cannot be Monitor as that would involve a conflict of interest with its duty to keep foundation trusts viable. It equally cannot be the Healthcare Commission because, again, there would be conflicts between independent oversight of standards and a duty to ensure that competition was effective. It would seem to require a third institution – an Ofhealth on the lines of Ofwat and Ofcom where these regulators both set the price for their market and act to deal with unfair competition within it.

16. The government, working with commissioners and regulators, must develop a failure regime for foundation trusts and NHS-run organisations: a piece of work that should have been completed more than a year ago.

17. PCTs need to evolve, and evolve fairly rapidly, into primarily commissioning bodies, performance managed by SHAs and the NHS commissioner. This should not preclude them from retaining some direct provision, with a clear Chinese wall between the provision and purchasing side. Nor, in the longer term, should it prevent them from creating directly managed operations to plug gaps in service, or to ensure continuity of care where a service fails. As far as possible, however, such arrangements should be temporary and subject to regular market testing. In other words, they should retain a role as provider of last resort.

18. Practice-based commissioning needs to move as soon as possible to real budgets. At this level, however, a pure purchaser/provider split is not possible. Practices are service providers, but by their referrals (even with patient choice) they remain commissioners of care. Where they introduce new services they will be, in effect, both commissioners and providers. They remain, however, small profitmaking businesses.

Where they wish to commission new services from themselves rather than from external providers, they should be subject to regulatory oversight and a potential veto by PCTs to ensure that public money is being properly used.

19. Length of contracts, and whether they are negotiated nationally, regionally or locally, is not something that can be stipulated through central guidance. They are a matter for judgement. Where additional physical capacity costing large sums is needed, contracts will clearly need to be longer than where capital investment is minimal. The NHS commissioner, working with SHAs and PCTs, will need to take a view of:

- When (as with ISTCs and diagnostics) national negotiations can create a market or produce the best value – a mix of quality and price that does not necessarily mean the cheapest.
- When local contracts would best be combined into a regional one.
- When purchasing is best left to an entirely local decision at PCT and practice level.

20. The commissioner will need to take the precautionary approach of any sensible private sector buyer of being careful to maintain a range of alternative suppliers, avoiding the risk of subjecting NHS purchasers to monopolies.

21. Once PCTs understand their role as commissioners, they should be open to approaches from any source for better ways to organise care – whether from practices, NHS trusts, private providers or voluntary providers.

22. Although the new market involves a degree of competition, such approaches may well involve collaboration between different sectors to produce innovative forms of care. There should, for example, be no bar on foundation trusts working with independent sector providers, nor on foundation trusts extending out into what in the past has been classified as primary or community care. Indeed one of the aims of the new commissioning system should be to destroy traditional concepts of primary and secondary care. Commissioners will need to examine each case on its merits, while retaining future contestability. If local monopolies of care do emerge, PCTs will be able to go to the economic regulator to have them broken up.

23. In the longer term, the working group favours turning PCTs into competing commissioners, with patients able to choose their commissioner. That, however, requires a lot of work as outlined above, as well as ways of retaining needs assessment and public health measures within the commissioning role.

24. In the shorter term, however, and in part to address the 'democratic deficit', PCTs should be given the 'membership councils' that have been created for foundation trusts. Indeed it would be better if this 'voice' element was removed from foundation trusts, as they are essentially healthcare providers, and placed solely with PCTs. They are the commissioners for their local communities and the place where the patient voice should be heard. If and when recommendation 23 is implemented, such membership councils will not be needed. Patient choice would replace them.

25. For commissioning to work well, some measures to create a more level playing field with regard to tax and contracting rules is needed between existing and emerging healthcare providers.

26. To have the flexibility to compete with the private and voluntary sectors, the section 11 consultation on changes of service for NHS organisations needs to be revised and its time scales reduced. Some rationalisation is also needed of the plethora of patient forums at PCT and trust level, and of the ability of local authority Oversight and Scrutiny Committees to intervene.

27. Independent sector providers, as well as those interested in taking on a commissioning role, need to work with the NHS to improve its commissioning skills. In the short term, improving commissioning may make life more difficult for the independent sector. In the long run, however, it is an essential investment. Without skilled commissioners a poor-quality market, with poor quality for patients, is virtually guaranteed, with the result that the whole concept of a supplier market would fall into disrepute.

28. Issues of competition and cross-subsidy involving charities and voluntary organizations need to be addressed in the longer term.

29. NHS and independent sector organisations need to make the success of the NHS IT programme a top priority. Both need to recognise that this will involve their own investment in training and infrastructure above the applications and services being provided by the national programme. Without high-quality IT both patient safety and financial performance will be at risk.

30. Boards of NHS-run organisations need to strengthen their financial skills. All those appointed to them need to understand that they are not there as representatives of sectional interests. They are there to focus on the organization's purpose: the outcomes produced for patients.

31. In time the tariff will almost certainly become a 'benchmark' price, rather than one that cannot be negotiated downwards, or one where elements of it cannot be negotiated upwards. For example, as it is disaggregated, that should allow providers from whichever sector to offer better and more cost effective packages of care – in which some elements may be above tariff, some below, but where the whole can be shown to offer better quality and value for money.

32. For long-term conditions there is an urgent need to disaggregate the tariff to achieve the objectives of the recent White Paper on care outside hospital.

33. The government should undertake a review of the need for continued national pay bargaining in the NHS.

34. The NHS, the independent sector, the royal colleges and others that oversee training and research and development, such as the Clinical Research Collaborative, need to develop programmes to allow both training and research and development to take place across the sectors.

The people involved in the working group are listed below:

Chair of Working Group – Greg Parston, Chairman, OPM and Director, Priory Group
Report editor – Nicholas Timmins, Public Policy Editor, *Financial Times*
Secretary – Tabitha Brufal, King's Fund
Facilitators – Nicholas Bradbury and Val Martin, Leadership Development, King's Fund

Working group members are in bold
Victor Adebowale, Chief Executive, Turning Point
Ken Anderson, Commerical Director, Department of Health
Zenna Atkins, Chairman, Portsmouth City Teaching PCT
Mark Bassett, Head of Public Policy, BUPA
Nicholas Beazley, Group Strategy Director, BUPA
Andy Black, Independent Consultant
Jonathan Boulton, Consultant Opthalmologist, RUH, Bath
Liz Bowsher, Branch Head of Planning & Performance Policy, Department of Health

John Chapman, Partner, Bevan Brittan
Chris Clough, Consultant Neurologist, King's Hospital and RCP
Robert Creighton, Chief Executive, Ealing PCT
Mike Farrar, Chief Executive West Yorkshire SHA
Mark Goldman, Chief Executive, Heart of England Foundation Trust
Neil Goodwin, Chief Executive, Greater Manchester SHA
Anne Heast, Director of Health, Tribal Group plc
Tom Hughes-Hallett, Chief Executive, Marie Curie
Alasdair Liddell, Independent Consultant and member of Ealing LIFT Co
Tommy MacDonald Miller, Director, Capio Nightingale Hospitals
Eric McCullogh, Chief Executive, National Association of Primary Care
Laurie McMahon, Co-founder, OPM
Monica McSharry, Chief Executive, North East London SHA
Alison Norman, Director of Nursing, Marie Curie
Keith Palmer, Senior Associate, King's Fund
Ali Parsaa, Clinical Centres of Excellence
Sylvie Pearce, Building Better Health
John Proctor, Pfizer
Carolyn Regan, Chief Executive, North East London SHA
Rebecca Rosen, Senior Fellow, King's Fund and General Practitioner
Stephen Sears, Chief Executive, Ealing Community Transport
Fay Selvan, Chair, Trafford PCT and Chief Executive, Big Life Group
Michael Shaw, Chief Executive, John Grooms
Ian Smith, Chief Executive, General Healthcare Group
Matthew Young, Public Policy Projects, Adam Smith Institute

At one level it is encouraging that such a mixed group, comprising people from the private, public and voluntary sectors, could come up with such consensus. At another level, though, the people who were invited to be in this working group from the NHS are very unusual in their open-mindedness. The norm in the NHS, as I explore in more detail below, are either opposed to change, or not competent to manage it – or both.

Civil Service involvement

The architects of failure are career NHS/Civil Service managers. The injection of new blood into the NHS/Civil Service is fiercely resisted by the protectionist incumbents. It is unlikely that those people who are

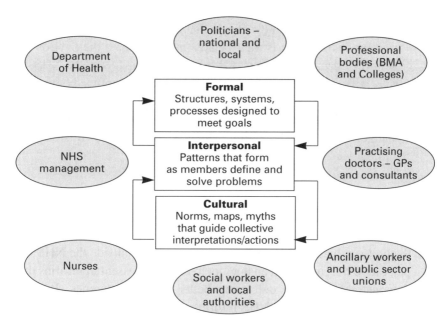

Figure 4.11   A complex cultural and behavioural cocktail

responsible for the mess can turn things around. Even if they were minded to do so, they have no experience of change management. They know how to work within the Disneyland of Whitehall and Westminster, and how to succeed in the warped world of NHS politics. But the 'catch 22' is that these are not, then, the people who can see that the 'Emperor has no clothes' – they have succeeded by working within the NHS and maintaining its status quo. Reform will stutter, at best, until fresh management is brought into the senior NHS ranks.

The NHS is a very complex environment (see Figure 4.11). Culture change is urgently required, and it will come from:

- A data-driven analysis of the problem, including an understanding that it is individual behaviours (more so than organization structures or abstract cultural characteristics) – *especially of senior managers* – that underpin the dysfunction. Many people feel themselves to be victims of a dysfunctional organization such as the NHS – but the fact is that organizations are made up of individuals, and it is their behaviours that create the environment they decry. In other words it is the participants in the NHS, especially senior managers, who are the architects of its dysfunction.

- Working with leaders in the various sub-groups to lead behaviour change. This underscores the call made elsewhere in this book for new leadership throughout the system.

It is ironic that it is accusations of 'privatization' that doctors' organizations, trade unions, reform-blocking middle and upper management, and the philosophically opposed minority inside and outside the NHS use as a pejorative rallying cry in an attempt to block the essential reforms that are demonstrably already delivering better patient outcomes. But the opposite is true – unless the NHS reforms, unless it starts giving patients high-quality medical care, and spends taxpayers' money efficiently, citizens will increasingly demand to be allowed to spend their own money on the healthcare that they choose. This will create a two-tier system. And the only way to prevent this outcome is to reform the system, and keep citizens engaged with it.

Being a self-perpetuating oligarchy, or a protected monopoly provider of health services to the citizens of Britain, is not and never was an objective of the NHS. It is not, and never was, a guiding principle of public service. It cannot be a foundation for an effective, patient-needs-centred service that delivers the best patient outcomes.

With all the reforms and all the initiatives, it is a natural human reaction to plead for a respite from more policy. And yet, there is justice in these calls. The more the system fails, the more politicians do what they do best – come up with more policy. But more policy, pumped into an unreformed bureaucracy, creates confusion. And this confusion is driving the calls for less change. This confusion and wasted effort is further compounded by the constant reorganizations that characterize bureaucracies. Constant reorganizations that change nothing are a hallmark of bureaucracies – it makes them feel as if they are doing something. The problem, though, is not change – it is that change has not addressed the dysfunctional organization and poor-quality management.

The stakes are very high. Unless we can reform the NHS behemoth, then British patients are going to suffer, and British taxpayers are going to have their taxes wasted. But the stakes go beyond the NHS. If reform of the NHS fails, there will be little chance that reform of the public sector more broadly will be successful. The UK will then be stuck with a high-cost public sector that continues to consider its interests to be paramount, while giving shoddy service to British citizens.

But if we get it right in the NHS, and manage to reform the public sector more broadly, we can achieve the vision outlined by the American authors, Osborne and Gaebler:

> Today's environment demands institutions that are extremely flexible and adaptable. It demands institutions that deliver high-quality goods and services, squeezing ever more bang out of every buck. It demands institutions that are responsive to their customers, offering choices of non-standardized services; that lead by persuasion and incentives rather than commands; that give their employees a sense of meaning and control, even ownership. It demands institutions that *empower* citizens rather than simply serving them . . . Our information technologies and our knowledge economy give us opportunities to do things we never dreamed possible 50 years ago. But to seize these opportunities, we must pick up the wreckage of our industrial-era institutions and re-build.[22]

5

Creating sustainability and building international competitiveness

Key points

1   The move from the NHS monolith to a real market that serves patients and citizens requires the creation of market mechanisms that will 'animate' the system and eliminate the need for central diktat. The key mechanisms are:

    1.1   Information (especially on patient value) that patients and commissioners can use to choose between alternative providers – on the basis of which one produces the best clinical outcomes.

    1.2   'Alternative Providers' means that competition has to be unconstrained – this will transform the NHS from being a huge, self-interested bureaucracy into a market that provides value to consumers (patients).

2   The radical reform agenda outlined in this book will not only benefit patients (by giving them a better service) and taxpayers (by giving them more value for money), but it will also make the country wealthier.

3   A competitive, patient-centred internal market will also make the UK competitive in international markets, and that will bring economic benefits to the country.

4   However, a patient-centred internal market is not enough – the key players have to start cooperating in new ways. The work of Michael Porter on healthcare was the core topic of Chapter 3. His earlier work on National Competitiveness provides the model for rebuilding the UK's international competitiveness in healthcare.

Creating sustainable market mechanisms in UK healthcare

Commissioners are the key to sustainability. They are the market-makers.

- Commissioners ensure that all services are put out to tender regularly (in natural monopolies) or that sufficient competition is maintained to keep organizations honest – in terms of keeping them focused on delivering high-quality services cost-efficiently. It is one of the unfortunate truisms that organizations – public or private – will try to build monopoly power if they can. It makes life much easier for them. Yet the difference is that, in the private sector, while most companies try to do this, it is recognized as being an immoral act that will compromise the rights of consumers, and there are increasingly effective legal and institutional processes that prevent abuse of consumer rights. But in the public sector, self-serving monopolies are viewed as being moral – public service is congruent with a public-sector monopoly. This is a massive confidence trick played on patients and taxpayers.
- At the other extreme, commissioners need to ensure that the markets are not too fragmented, and that, as a consequence, economies of scale and scope are not deployed in the best interests of the patient. The NHS is a paradox, in that it is monolithic, but also highly fragmented, as each local Trust is not allowed to expand outside its small patch. Economies of scale (in terms of building deep competence in treating specific medical conditions) and scope (taking this greater and safer competence to all parts of the country) are therefore not exploited in the interests of patients.
- Commissioners make sure that market failure does not interrupt service to the public. This is largely achieved by making sure that the previous point works. Competition will allow patients to move to better providers. In natural monopolies, as service fails, then the commissioners need to have 'substitutes' ready to step in. As clinical units – most probably within Foundation Trust organizations – become national and build replicable competencies, so they will be ready to step in. Opponents of competition say that market failure is not acceptable. What they miss, of course, is that failure is occurring all the time in the current NHS.

> The Bristol Royal Infirmary scandal persisted for years. The consequence of monopolies is that failure becomes trapped within the system – there are no mechanisms to identify them quickly enough and root them out. Failure is endemic in the monopolistic NHS – it will only be healed if competition, managed by the commissioners – is unleashed.

Regulation is essential to make sure that any economy runs well, and that consumers are protected. A new regulator (or perhaps the role could be filled by Monitor, the organization run by Bill Moyes) would define the role of commissioners and oversee, as guardians of the public good, their market-making activities. This market regulator would be the champion of patient choice.

The other major regulatory role would be to collect and publish patient outcomes – and to alert the market regulator if patient safety is endangered. This is the role of the Healthcare Commission. They should be the champions of patient safety.

The NHS's role in the decline of the UK as a world leader in healthcare and biomedical science

Perhaps one of the most depressing aspects of the failure of NHS organization and management is the effect on innovation. From being one of the most successful and innovative healthcare economies in the world, the UK is now derided by the other developed nations. In order that the NHS can become once more a leader in innovation, then the final part of the puzzle is for a way to be found of restoring the UK's leadership in biomedical science. This is the topic of the final section of this book.

The UK used to be a world leader in medical research and in the application of that research to better patient outcomes. We were the well-spring of the molecular revolution, the source of discovery and use of ultrasound, MRI and much more besides. In the early days of the NHS, we had a virtuous circle in that a high reputation for research and clinical practice both encouraged the best people into the profession and, when inside the profession, these people competed with each other to be the best, both in the UK and in the world.

This created a motivated clinical workforce who were very engaged in the three major institutions that drove the profession forward:

- The universities
- The Royal Colleges
- The hospitals

This integrated and engaged clinical workforce fed into high performance and contributed to a high and well-earned reputation for research and clinical practice. But, this virtuous circle has begun to unravel since the early 1990s. As NHS managers, with no knowledge or experience of research or its impact on clinical practice, took over control of hospitals, the crucial link between academic leadership and clinical excellence was lost.

The system has lost the ability to create bespoke organizations, expecting small rural PCTs to have the same governance structures as major international research organizations such as the Hammersmith Hospital. The Royal Colleges gradually gave up their influence on the teaching agenda and the teaching curriculum got taken over by NHS bureaucrats and social scientists.

A once-virtuous circle has now become a vicious circle: fragmented research and a poor teaching environment have led to a loss of clinical excellence. As a result, morale has declined, and this has been compounded by poor management of the academic clinical workforce in the hospitals. The doctors have become disaffected and alienated, and disengaged from the management process and from controlling the teaching curriculum.

Julian Le Grand illustrated the deterioration of NHS innovation in an LSE lecture:

The NHS was poor on innovation. When I was working at No 10, I lost count of the number of times people came to me with often what seemed to be brilliant and innovative ideas, but incredibly frustrated by their inability to get the NHS even to try them out let alone adopt them across the service. Simply demonstrating good ideas or good practice or even publishing them were not sufficient: the incentives for adoption were not there.[1]

Diamonds and clusters

Today's vicious circle must be broken.

Reform has to start with the research and teaching agenda, entailing radical reform of the institutions themselves. The UK needs to establish academic medical centres with a governance framework that champions research and teaching as a means to excellence in patient care. These would build on the existing clinical research networks and would be required to match the altered care approach outlined in this book, where patient care is organized along patient care pathways and cuts across conventional primary and secondary care models.

Once the public sector monopoly has been broken down, the UK can begin to be more ambitious in how it builds international competence and competitiveness. The first step is to create more innovation and competition at the level of treatments. This in itself will stimulate research in the institutions that will enhance clinical practice which will in turn feed back to research, and so on. For this to happen:

- There needs to be more transparency, so that the medical profession as a whole can learn which treatments are most effective.
- Over time, chambers of doctors (building demonstrable clinical expertise in their speciality) will become better known, and the mechanism of patient choice will drive patients towards the better doctors.
- Clinical rewards will be system-wide as better treatments are publicized and copied.
- Clinical outcome data needs to be collected comprehensively, analysed objectively and published.

Institutions that clearly understand the two-way process that is medical research – from the bench to the bedside, and from clinical experience and observation to animal and cellular models – need to be created between the leading research universities and the NHS.

At the national level this has led to the publication of the Cooksey Review (2006: *A Review of UK Health Research Funding*, HMSO) which highlights the failure of the UK to invest in clinical research, but advocates the development of a new research body that will oversee clinical research funding.

At the local level, the creation of five new comprehensive biomedical research centres further enhances the position of clinical research. However, neither of these innovations will work unless the governance of these internationally competitive research hospitals recognizes the need to have research and teaching as a core function of their activity, and ensures that expertise in these areas is matched by the executive and non-executive teams responsible for running these organizations. Continuing to have hospitals run by individuals with no experience of research or teaching or clinical practice will ensure failure. If a new emphasis is placed on innovation, best practice and institutional change, the UK's medical reputation can be rebuilt.

The obstacles to replicating this success are a declining NHS and a dysfunctional system that fails to highlight the importance of research and teaching to the detriment of patient care. This decline in our medical competence is not only bad for the health of the nation but is also disastrous in terms of continuous clinical development and the nation's overall ability to create wealth.

A first step to a return to a virtuous circle would be to rationalize tertiary/academic bodies into a more coherent structure. But reorganization alone is not enough, and the objective should be to create internationally competitive competence clusters. Countries are not competitive in everything, and despite the rise of globalization; there still remains a strong geographical dimension to competitiveness. Michael Porter published a book called *The Competitive Advantage of Nations*,[2] which identified the cluster of competitiveness in a number of countries around the world. He developed a model, the 'Diamond' that explains how regions become internationally competitive. We shall describe this model in more detail below.

Porter's map of internationally competitive clusters in the USA is shown in Figure 5.1. Good examples of best practice outside the UK are established models such as the Harvard University, the University of Maryland and the Massachusetts Institute of Technology (MIT).

The contribution of the Boston region in Massachusetts was examined in a study in 2000. The results were summarized as follows:

- A $7.4 billion boost to the regional economy
- Work for 48,750 university employees and 37,000 other workers in the region, who pay millions of dollars in federal, state and local taxes
- A talent pool of more than 31,900 graduates, many of whom stay in the Boston area

184

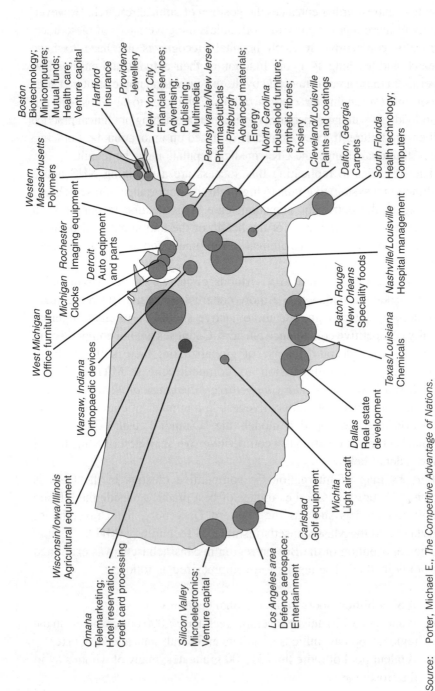

Source: Porter, Michael E., *The Competitive Advantage of Nations.*

Figure 5.1 Selected regional clusters of competitive industries

- Innovative research that resulted in 264 patents, 280 commercial licenses of technology, and 41 start-up companies
- Continuing education for 25,000 non-degree students
- Numerous programmes to help local K-12 schools and individual students
- Community improvements through construction of housing, streets, and increases in environmental benefits[3]

Companies such as Amgen, Cisco, Merck, Novartis, Pfizer and Sun Microsystems have located major facilities in the area, to gain access to the research universities and their affiliated hospital and research institutions concentrated in the Boston area. The university-affiliated hospitals and research centres alone received US$1 billion in grants and contracts to conduct research in 2000.

The universities in the Boston area are engaged very actively in aligning with the private sector. Some of the alliances have been/are:

- **Merck** – direct scientific collaboration on research into pharmaceuticals.
- **Ford Motor Company** – research with special emphasis on environmental and design challenges.
- **Nippon Telegraph & Telephone Corporation** – creating new technologies in telecommunications and computers.
- **Merrill Lynch** – to fund collaborative projects across a broad range of disciplines in financial engineering, technological innovation and management.
- **DuPont** – to develop processes for new materials directed at bioelectronics, biosensors, bio-mimetic materials, alternative energy sources and new high-value materials.
- **Microsoft** – to engage additional academic and industry partners and produce materials that can be published and disseminated widely.
- **Hewlett-Packard** – to develop innovative ways of creating and handling digital information.

The Boston region as a centre of excellence is based on the 'diamond' and 'cluster' concepts.

This deliberate approach to building excellence in biomedical science is to be found in a number of places around the USA. In 1996, for example, the University of Maryland formally adopted a plan, 'Charting a Path to Excellence: The Strategic Plan for the University of Maryland at College Park'. The idea of the plan was to outline a vision of academic excellence and set in motion strategic initiatives and guidelines for action.

By 2000, the University could claim that:

Our progress can be measured by our achievements in many areas.

- Innovative, effective and popular learning communities
- An expanding number of academic programmes of recognised distinction
- An increasingly productive engagement with the research, business and government communities
- Significant contributions through award-winning scholarships to the interpretation and preservation of history and culture
- Vibrant and growing creative and performing arts programmes
- Major contributions through nationally-recognised research in public policy, biology, physics, information science, technology and engineering; and innovative leadership in agricultural and natural resources[4]

The vehicle that drives its relationship to businesses, government and industry is its Office of Technology Commercialisation (OTC). OTC encourages the participation of the business, government and industry sectors through the technology transfer process, which focuses the university's research towards viable products that benefit the local, state and national economies.

Other centres of excellence in the Boston area include Harvard College, with its research centres, and Harvard Business School, which includes Michael Porter among its leading academics. The Harvard Business School's involvement in Silicon Valley is well documented. It can now compete on an international basis with global research centres in the Asia-Pacific rim, California and Europe.

The UK has to develop effective 'diamond' and cluster models. This cannot be achieved with the current governance of our leading hospitals that lack the academic and business leadership needed to make them internationally competitive. The logic is that countries are not competitive in all industries, but only in ones that have a good 'diamond' and where there are clusters of specialized and supporting industries.

In his book, Porter shows that competition between companies at the microeconomic level, is an important part of an effective 'diamond'. Where governments have 'picked winners' and then subsidized them, and where they have protected industries from competition (such as MITI famously did in Japan in the 1970s and 1980s), so these industries have, in almost all cases, failed. The need is *not*, then, some sort of collusion between biomedical centres in the UK. The best – Imperial College; University College London; King's College London; Universities of Oxford and Cambridge – will only succeed if they compete hard against each other. Only through competition will they strive to innovate and demonstrate excellence.

Notwithstanding the need for competition, there is the reverse problem in the UK. The 'egalitarianism' of the NHS mindset has meant that money has been directed to research institutions not based on performance, but on the basis of 'fair shares for all'. This has created a fragmented biomedical and research industry in the UK. Therefore, we need to see, simultaneously, consolidation of the industry in terms of more money going to the best (including absorption of the outliers into the 'orbit' of the best), *and* competition between the best centres.

The consolidation part of this simultaneous equation is described in the 'hub and spokes' model advocated by the Science and Technology Select Committee in its report on its inquiry into strategic science provision in English universities. Essentially, it said that universities that are centres of excellence should collaborate with other universities who were strong in some scientific areas, but weaker in others. The Select Committee could see the way that teaching could complement research, and vice versa; how different disciplines could help each other; and how this would be of benefit to the local and regional economy. As the Committee Report put it:

> The Lambert Review also identified a perceived bias within the university system towards research, meaning that 'instead of concentrating on their own areas of comparative advantage, which may be of real value to their local and regional economy – [universities] strive to be measured against a world-class benchmark . . . The collaborative model is commonplace in the United States. Several submissions made reference to this. Senior scientists from the pharmaceutical industry, for example, stated that, in the US, 'universities derive enough income

from teaching to fund undergraduate activities . . . Many of the smaller colleges are renowned for producing high quality graduates who often transfer to major research departments (e.g. Harvard, Columbia, Stanford, MIT, etc.) to pursue postdoctoral-level work'. The Director General of the Research Councils stated that 'looking at some of the private and state funded universities in the US, they are very proud to attract an extremely good core bench across Massachusetts, New Hampshire, and so on . . . Professor Ian Diamond (no relation to the model!) of RCUK emphasised that collaboration could even invigorate research taking place outside the main research hubs: 'where there are pockets of excellence and where there are particularly junior pockets of excellence we do try to enable there to be, for example, something like a hub and spokes model which has the best junior institutions able to be part of some of the critical mass of larger centres, particularly where there is expensive equipment that is required to be used to take forward research.[5]

The Select Committee concluded:

> The hub and spokes model of university provision would allow STEM departments to capitalise on their areas of strength, whether they are research, teaching or knowledge-transfer, whilst still ensuring that undergraduates received a rounded education in the discipline of their choice. By collaborating on their provision of STEM courses, departments would make more efficient use of resources, and thereby ease the financial difficulties currently being experienced by many STEM departments. We recommend that the Government encourages the acceptance and implementation of this model throughout the system via HEFCE, the RDAs and Universities UK, and by means of the funding regime for higher education.[6]

This is not a sterile academic argument, but has direct consequences for healthcare. Mortality ratios for UK hospitals (a measure of the chances of dying) show unequivocally that teaching hospitals are far safer than hospitals not linked to an academic environment. It is hard to find a more concrete example of the link between medical school teaching, biomedical research and improved patient outcomes. However, this type of collaboration is not easy in the notoriously jealous and protective world of the universities:

The only barrier to the realisation of the benefits to be conferred by the implementation of the hub and spokes model of provision is in the form of the universities themselves. Unless they collaborate with each other, it will not work. Forcing them to do so would be a breach of their autonomy. However, we have argued that the Government can, and already does, influence the choices that universities make by means of the funding regime. . . . The hub and spokes model of university provision would allow STEM departments to capitalise on the areas of strength, whether they are research, teaching or knowledge transfer, whilst still ensuring that undergraduates received a rounded education in the discipline of their choice.[7]

In December 2006 prime minister Tony Blair endorsed the first attempt by the UK to establish a global medical excellence cluster involving the five new biomedical research centres. The next section will go into more detail on the 'diamond' and cluster models.

A conceptual model for putting it right

In 1990, Michael Porter wrote *The Competitive Advantage of Nations,* a book on national competitiveness that has become highly influential. He outlined a conceptual model that explains why certain industries in certain countries/regions across the world became internationally competitive.

His model identifies four factors that interact (in a 'diamond') to build competitiveness. Contrary to conventional wisdom, despite the important globalization processes that are occurring, the home base and the impact of forces acting within a bounded geographical area are vital in building competitiveness. The 'diamond' is illustrated diagrammatically in Figure 5.2.

The four elements of the 'diamond' in healthcare are:

- Countries that have sophisticated home demand, where consumers are demanding, have higher levels of innovation. Companies respond to the 'tough' feedback that sophisticated consumers give them. In developing excellence in delivering goods and services to demanding customers, so companies are challenged to improve. Italians, for example, are very fashion-conscious, so it is no

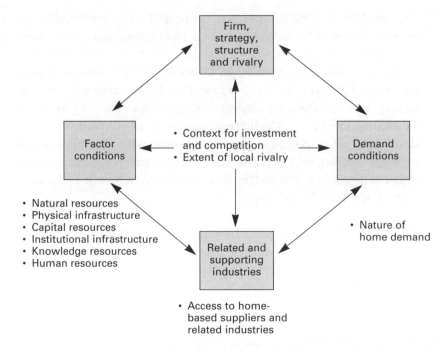

Source: Porter, Michael E., *The Competitive Advantage of Nations.*

Figure 5.2   Determinants of competitiveness

surprise that Italian companies have the dominant market share
in fashion across the world. In terms of healthcare reform in the
UK, this generic finding about demand conditions points to the
importance of demand-side mechanisms – primary care, patient
choice, measurement of clinical outcomes and commissioning –
discussed in the previous chapter.

• The second part of the 'diamond' is 'Factor Conditions'.
  Companies will be helped in becoming internationally competitive
  if the infrastructure within which they operate is well developed.
  Traditionally, this has meant physical infrastructure (in terms of a
  good transport system, or high investment in capital equipment,
  for example) and financial infrastructure (the availability and
  liquidity of capital). These are still important, but more important
  are human and knowledge assets. In terms of UK healthcare, the
  increased spending of the early 1990s, and the greater investment

in technology, is improving the physical infrastructure. However, the medical teaching and training agenda is not very well advanced. A major theme of this final chapter is the need for the UK to restore its position as one of the best places (if not *the* best) in the world in which to train for, and practice, medicine.

- Competition between competent institutions is essential if a region is to develop international excellence. Protected and pampered industries and institutions do not thrive. A regulatory environment that prevents both extreme fragmentation and monopoly abuse is essential. The theme of this book is that the NHS is a monopoly, and we need to see it broken down so that patients and clinicians – rather than the public-sector unions and civil servants – can be the beneficiaries of the system, and so that the UK can regain its leadership in biomedical science.

- In economically successful regions, companies within an industry sector 'cluster' together, creating a rich, interconnecting dynamic. Sweden, for example, is internationally competitive in paper production. This is based on a rich and deep cluster of related and supporting industries (and academic institutions specialized in various aspects of forestry and wood-products manufacturing). The same principle holds in biomedical science. In order to rebuild the UK's competitive position, we need to engineer this richness and interconnectivity back into the centres of clinical excellence. We have to reverse the tired decline in excellence that centralized state ownership of the NHS monopoly is producing. On the foundations of excellence in clinical practice, we need to build clusters of related and supporting research in both universities and industries, encompassing the new patient-centred NHS, medical technology companies, pharmaceutical companies, academic institutions, engineering research and scientific (especially genetic) research.

Monitor Company (not connected to the regulator of Foundation Trusts) has provided the 'organizing context' for a number of 'cluster studies' to build its competitiveness in medical practice and biomedical science. The example shown in Figure 5.3 is taken from the Life Sciences cluster in New Jersey, USA.

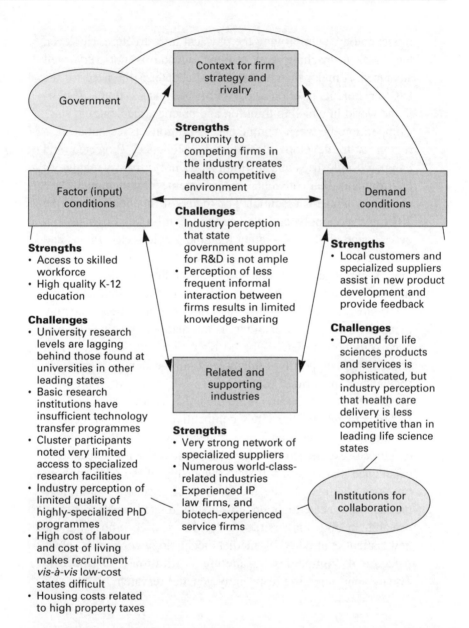

Government

Context for firm strategy and rivalry

Strengths
- Proximity to competing firms in the industry creates health competitive environment

Challenges
- Industry perception that state government support for R&D is not ample
- Perception of less frequent informal interaction between firms results in limited knowledge-sharing

Factor (input) conditions

Strengths
- Access to skilled workforce
- High quality K-12 education

Challenges
- University research levels are lagging behind those found at universities in other leading states
- Basic research institutions have insufficient technology transfer programmes
- Cluster participants noted very limited access to specialized research facilities
- Industry perception of limited quality of highly-specialized PhD programmes
- High cost of labour and cost of living makes recruitment *vis-à-vis* low-cost states difficult
- Housing costs related to high property taxes

Demand conditions

Strengths
- Local customers and specialized suppliers assist in new product development and provide feedback

Challenges
- Demand for life sciences products and services is sophisticated, but industry perception that health care delivery is less competitive than in leading life science states

Related and supporting industries

Strengths
- Very strong network of specialized suppliers
- Numerous world-class-related industries
- Experienced IP law firms, and biotech-experienced service firms

Institutions for collaboration

Source: Monitor analysis of in-depth interviews and online survey of key industry, academic and government leaders, October–December 2002. New Jersey Life Sciences Super Cluster Initiative, Survey Results – Princeton, New Jersey, 14 February 2003. Reproduced with permission http://www.isc.hbs,edu/pdf/NJ_Lifescience.pdf

Figure 5.3   Summary of the business environment of the New Jersey life sciences super-cluster

Health and wealth

Rebuilding the UK's competitiveness in biomedical science is going to take time. Towards the end of this chapter I outline a project to create Britain's first such cluster, the global medical excellence cluster (GMEC). Some useful work that will inform that project was done in 2001 by the Association of British Healthcare Industries (ABHI). That body commissioned a report to answer the question, 'How can the UK create, retain and grow a greater proportion of the added value of the world's healthcare?' The objectives of the report were to recommend ways in which the UK could:

- Be a highly innovative sector capable of creating new and better products which have a global competitive advantage and embedding them in UK resident business
- Be a conducive environment for growth of current established businesses
- Be an attractive operating base for the value adding activities of foreign companies (foreign companies currently dominate most of the market sectors in the UK and internationally)[8]

A map of the UK healthcare sector

The ABHI report drew a map of the UK healthcare sector, which included the following points:

- The UK constitutes about 3% of world healthcare expenditure compared to 43% in the USA, 11% in Japan, 8% in Germany and 29% for the EU as a whole.
- Healthcare expenditure per capita in the UK is low compared with other OECD countries. At the time of the 1998 international comparisons, the UK was close to the bottom of the OECD league tables of capita expenditure on health (6.7% GDP).
- The UK has the lowest share of healthcare expenditure contributed by the private sector (15% compared with an OECD average of 28%). It is almost unique in having a nationalised health service, the NHS, in which payer and provider are the same organisation (the UK Government). The role of private/independent hospitals and clinics and of insurance companies in the UK is atypically small. In

1999, private acute hospitals had a total turnover of £3 billion compared to a total NHS expenditure of £52 billion. The UK insurance companies had a total turnover in medical business of circa £2.3 billion. However, long term care of the elderly is dominated by private and voluntary provision and there is a newly emerging subsector of private firms providing medical care support at home.

- The UK market for healthcare technologies is about 3% of the global market. Spending on healthcare technology per capita in the UK is half, or less than half, that of the most advanced markets of North America, Switzerland, Scandinavia and Germany.
- Analysis of sub-sectors of the market shows a concentration of market share in leading international companies. The top 15% of players account for about 80% market share in each of the defined market sub-sectors. Tighter market segmentation would show less than five significant players in each segment. The UK market structure is a microcosm of the world market. The leading international companies in each sub-sector of the global market tend to have international turnovers of £1 billion per annum or more. Leading pharmaceutical companies have sales in excess of £5 billion per annum.

The report went on to argue that:

The presence of large, internationally effective companies in the UK is vital to the strength of the sector, not only for the value they generate in sales and employment but because:

- They lead significant supply networks
- They have global reach
- They have capacity to interact with, and absorb technology from, the science base
- They can spin out new companies in their non-core areas
- They can acquire and consolidate new companies in their core areas
- They train staff who can become part of the sector's knowledge pool[9]

The NHS is the world's single largest healthcare delivery organisation. The relationship between the NHS, as the major home customer, and UK based firms is of critical importance to the capacity to develop clinically effective and cost-effective solutions.

In other words, the ABHI makes the same point as the one made earlier in this chapter, that the dysfunction of the NHS not only harms patient's interests; it makes us all poorer. The ABHI report went on to discuss the benefits of having a vibrant biomedical industry in the UK:

> Healthcare is an important business and information technologies will play an increasingly important role in enabling improvements in quality and cost-effectiveness of care. Hardware includes generic equipment (e.g. tele-communications, servers, data warehouses, personal computers), call and alarm systems and a wide range of healthcare-specific equipment to deliver remote medicine and remote care. Software includes generic software and healthcare-specific software systems to deliver administrative support, clinical/pathology and diagnostic services, electronic prescribing and electronic patient records. There is also a growing opportunity for the development of decision support systems for patients and clinicians. It has been difficult to value the total business as a large proportion of the hardware and software is generic.[10]

The report also stressed another point made earlier in this book – that we need to develop medical education, and that the key to an improving healthcare system in the UK is reform of the NHS:

> Education and training are key to the continuous development of the wide range of skills needed to deliver healthcare. There are about 9,000 students studying medicine in the UK and a 57% expansion is planned. There are also about 30,000 students studying subjects allied to medicine. Developments in IT are opening new opportunities for delivery of continuing professional education and a number of specialist education companies are being formed . . . Government, through the Department of Health, plays a dominant role in the UK healthcare sector as policy maker, regulator, payer, deliverer of care, prime customer for the supply industry and as official sponsoring department for the industry at home and abroad. The relationship between governments and the private sector is key to the success of the NHS and of the suppliers.[11]

Constraints to growth for UK-based companies

One of the major objectives of the ABHI report was to identify the constraints to growth of UK-based healthcare technology companies, both in the UK market and internationally. To that end, a questionnaire was sent to 4,600 firms, of which 500 replied. The question was, 'What are the three major constraints to your growth in (a) the UK market; and (b) the international market?'

The biggest single influence on competitive advantage in the UK market was seen as the behaviour of the home 'customer' (the NHS). Innovative customers working in partnership with suppliers result in innovative businesses in innovative supply networks. Regressive customers produce weak suppliers.

As the ABHI report put it:

> The most important message in the report is that the health of the dominant UK customer, the NHS and that of the UK healthcare technology businesses are intimately dependent on each other. The UK suppliers and the various agencies of the NHS which seek to achieve improvements in clinical effectiveness and cost-effectiveness need to work together more closely to the potential benefit of companies, the NHS and patients.[12]

Doing business with the NHS is like dealing with a Third-World country. Indeed, in many cases, NHS managers even refuse to meet people from the private sector. Clinicians have similar stories to tell about the incompetence of NHS management.

Other UK market constraints included: 'The most important internal corporate constraints to growth were . . . shortages of key resources, notably of skilled people and finance.'

As well as the behaviour and structure of the NHS, the other constraints identified by ABHI were:

- The second most important constraint . . . in the business environment category, to exports was seen to be regulation. This included lack of harmonisation of regulation and lack of even handed application of rules where harmonisation officially existed.
- A lack of scale and shortage of resources were seen to be the major internal constraint to developing international business. Most companies are small and do not have either the skill set or the time to understand and service overseas markets adequately and profitably.
- Establishing effective networks between UK suppliers and foreign end-customers was seen as a major difficulty. There were strongly

expressed issues reflecting: (a) difficulties in finding appropriate distributors; (b) the level of commitment and priority given by those distributors to creating the market for the UK companies' products; and (c) the added costs and risks of operating in a longer supply chain.

The ABHI report drew a number of conclusions that are broadly in line with the thinking in this chapter:

The key to the successful growth of UK companies in world markets lies in:

- Innovation to gain competitive advantage over existing players or open new market segments.
- The ability to create products of sufficient potential to attract the development and marketing resources necessary to succeed internationally.
- Sufficient competitive advantage to be attractive partners in supply networks.[13]

The companies that will drive the growth of the UK's overall market share are either:

- Large, established, innovative players (few in number and well known).
- Innovative 'middle market' companies (with turnover greater than £5 million a year); often dominant players in a niche market or suppliers of key components.
- Early stage companies with a very significant new source of competitive advantage.

A critical factor affecting the success of firms developing innovative products will be the ability of the NHS to become an innovative early customer:

- The NHS would gain in productivity through pursuit of clinical effectiveness and cost-effectiveness.
- UK industry would have a home market test bed that enabled the necessary reference markets for international sales.
- Patients would get a better service.

The scale of the NHS and the international reputation of UK medical research and practice is a valuable national asset which could be harnessed to greater effect.

To achieve the objective it (the NHS) must:

- Be a highly innovative sector capable of creating new and better products which have a global competitive advantage and embedding them in UK resident business.
- Be a conducive environment for growth of current established businesses.
- Be a stimulating environment in which to start new, innovative healthcare businesses.

The conclusion on the relationship between the healthcare industry and the NHS illustrates how far the NHS has declined over the years, and how far the UK's international competitiveness has been undermined:

The historical relationship between the healthcare technology suppliers and the NHS, described in this [the ABHI] report, has not been driven by a shared vision of patient centred care with clinical effectiveness and cost-effectiveness as the measurable 'bottom line'. It has often been driven by short-term cost minimisation and risk-averse management.

Internationally, innovative companies have focused on other national markets where rewards to innovation are greater. However, the nation has most of the building blocks to move forward if there is a common will.[14]

The ABHI report argues that the government can only make a significant impact on two areas: the behaviour of the home customer and the business environment. As they put it:

The NHS should:

- Embrace clinical effectiveness and cost-effectiveness as major objectives.
- Involve the supply industry more openly in seeking whole system solutions, considering care pathways as well as organisational dimensions.

- Align process improvement strategies with purchasing policy.[15]
- Disseminate best practice.
  - ○ Best, or perhaps better, practice can be found in many places; internationally and within the NHS. Some is recorded in the NHS Beacon programme. Some is hidden from view. The NHS should:
    - Work to make best practice more visible.
    - Openly reward best practice.
    - Work to create an innovation culture.
- Assess cost-effectiveness. The lack of evidence for cost-effectiveness hampers product development and marketing by firms and adoption by the NHS. This is NOT an argument for randomised controlled trials on everything or full academic reviews before anything is done.
- The NHS and industry should work together to establish:
  - ○ Simple cost-effective processes for assessing cost-effectiveness.
  - ○ Suitable metrics for developing the longer term evidence base from practical application of products and processes.

  These would both inform 'best' practice in the UK and give UK firms the evidence for international marketing.
- Introduce business friendly purchasing. The NHS should review purchasing policy against criteria of
  - ○ Promotion of innovation
  - ○ Speed of decision making (poor cash flow kills companies).

  It could also simplify purchasing for both itself and business by driving a more rationalised and tiered supply network, learning from the aerospace and automotive industries.

On the issue of the business environment, the ABHI report concluded:

- The healthcare sector is no exception in wanting a reduced burden of general regulation and 'innovation friendly' specific healthcare regulation. The UK needs to continue to influence international regulations as strongly as possible and minimise the burden at home.
- There should also be greater emphasis on incentives for the private sector to pull innovation from public sector research, rather than expect the public sector to push innovation out. This requires better linkage between the Department of Health, DTI and business, and the development of mechanisms akin to the US SBIR (Small Business Innovation and Research) system.

The NHS, without the reforms outlined in this book, will not embrace clinical effectiveness and cost effectiveness as major objectives. It will not contribute to building the UK's international competitiveness in health-care and, as a consequence, without reform, it will continue to fail patients and taxpayers, and will continue to impoverish the country.

Global medical excellence clusters

In the next decade, five or six global medical excellence clusters will drive medical innovation, state-of-the-art medical treatment, and train the next generation of doctors. They will be characterized by:

- World-class institutions (including universities, hospitals, pharmaceutical and medical device companies)
- A strong global reputation to attract resources and high-calibre talent
- A shared vision for excellence
- Principles and structures to ensure effective collaboration

The most established medical excellence cluster is in Boston and Cambridge in Massachusetts. Singapore, Shanghai, New Delhi and Dubai clusters are in the process of being built. The most established medical excellence cluster is the Boston Cambridge Triangle, with two world-renowned universities, eight medical schools, fourteen teaching hospitals with 15,000 staff, and more than 200 life science companies. The focus of the Boston and Cambridge cluster is research, product development and improved patient care. It has a dominant position in medical innovation, registering more than 10,000 medical patents a year (compared to 1,000 patents in London), and conducts more than 1,500 product clinical trials. The centre also provides world-class patient care to more than 2 million domestic patients, and an additional 6,000 international patients. Life science companies contribute to the local economy, providing more than 90,000 jobs.

The US West Coast Axis covers Stanford Medical School and the bioscience innovation companies around Stanford, as well as the cluster of universities and bioscience companies in Los Angeles. Its focus is on research, product development and the incubation of new bioscience companies. The Bay Area alone has 820 life science companies and employs 250,000 people, directly and indirectly.

Strong government support is driving the creation of global medical excellence clusters in Singapore, Shanghai, New Delhi and Dubai:

- Singapore's government is funding and co-ordinating efforts to strengthen Singapore as a global and regional medical excellence cluster. The focus is on both research and patient care. Singapore invested US$600 million in 2005 in stem cell research, with a goal of attracting more than 1 million international patients by 2012 (up from 200,000 in 2006).
- Shanghai is investing US$1.2 billion to build a 'medical zone' and adopting a similar model to the US West Coast Axis, focused on research and product development. The aim is to create world-class facilities and links to foreign partners to develop a dominant position in key medical technologies through co-ordinated government and commercial activity. The ability of China to position itself as a leading player – for example, in the anti-infective sector – demonstrates the commitment and impact of the Chinese approach to building an ability to compete globally in high-technology areas.
- New Delhi's focus is on attracting international patients to world-class facilities by offering treatment at lower cost and with shorter waiting times than in the USA or Europe. The aim is to generate US$2 billion from overseas patients by 2012.
- Dubai is pursuing a similar strategy to New Delhi, and funding a 4.1m sq ft complex to form an 'internationally recognized location of choice for quality healthcare and an integrated centre of excellence for clinical and wellness service, medical education and research'. In order to strengthen its reputation, Dubai is working in partnership with Harvard Medical School to develop its capabilities.

The starting point for building a global medical excellence cluster is a set of world-class institutions with strong reputations to attract and retain high-calibre medical professionals and draw in funding. The world-class institutions need to be clustered in close proximity, within a 45–60-minute travel radius. In Boston and Cambridge there are two leading research centres, at Harvard Medical School and Massachusetts Institute of Technology (MIT), and three world-class hospitals: Massachusetts General (MGH); Brigham and Women's Teaching Hospital; and the Beth Israel/Deaconess Hospital. The catchment area also includes leading pharmaceutical and device companies (for example, Novartis, Fresenius, Becton Dickinson, Medtronic, Genzyme and Boston Scientific).

To compete internationally it is critical that the institutions build global reputations in expertise in specific medical areas. The Boston Cambridge Triangle has targeted its resources on a limited number of specialties and attracted through its 'Partners in Healthcare' programme fourteen Nobel laureates. Over 25 per cent of PhD students are from overseas, and a significant proportion stay on after completing their studies to join research centres within the city. In addition, the Boston Cambridge Triangle attracts more than 20 per cent of US venture capital investment.

The second characteristic of a global medical excellence cluster is a framework of goals, principles and institutions that encourages and facilitates collaborative behaviour and individual institutional excellence. Successful clusters commit to a set of goals focused on global competitiveness; on building capabilities to lead in specific fields of R&D, and on developing the ability to attract key talent and funds from both national and international organizations (including major pharmaceutical companies and institutions such as the Gates Foundation).

Leading clusters have put significant emphasis on developing and embedding a set of principles to ensure effective collaboration. These principles include:

- Recognition of the existence of common areas of interest
- Criticality of extensive networks to facilitate communication
- Need for open access to the cluster with no institutions being excluded but with the principle that excellence is the basis of collaboration
- Importance of structuring collaborative activities to achieve specific goals rather than collaboration being an end in itself
- The necessity of specialization within the cluster to reduce destructive competition

- Acceptance that competition between institutions is important to improve individual performance as long as it does not damage the overall performance of the cluster

Medical excellence clusters also require a limited number of institutions to facilitate and guide collaboration. These include the appointment of a programme chairperson to advise participants in the cluster and to act as a catalyst to encourage cross-organizational activities. Their role also includes the management of external parties and building the global reputation of the cluster. It is also useful to set up working parties to drive specific initiatives and to agree priorities for research. Finally, it is also critical to set up networking organizations to facilitate communication. In Boston and Cambridge, 'Partners in Healthcare' brings leading physicians in contact with patients and research opportunities, and the Centre for Integration of Medicine and Innovative Technology links universities and research centres with industry.

The UK has all the institutions to become a major global medical excellence cluster, but lacks the necessary co-ordinating framework. Many of the existing initiatives (for example, The Medical Research Council (MRC), National Institute for Health Research, London Development Agency Life Sciences Strategy and Action plan) focus only on a limited number of stakeholders. They do not provide effective mechanisms to co-ordinate across the cluster's universities, teaching hospitals, industry and government. More work is required to build a set of principles to improve collaboration and produce more tangible results from joint initiatives. There is a need to set targets and ambitions with a more global perspective.

The UK will fall behind if no action is taken. Global competition for medical professionals and resources will increase, and over time funds will flow to other centres so it will be difficult to retain key personnel. Loss of competitiveness will have an adverse impact on research, product development and the UK's ability to continually improve standards of patient care in certain key disease areas. The opportunity will be missed to exploit both the medical and economic potential of the UK's assets.

The UK requires a programme to develop a common vision and framework to build a global medical excellence cluster.

To this end, the South East England Medical Excellence Cluster (GMEC) was established at the beginning of 2007 to leverage London and the south east region's unique combination of world-class medical universities, pharmaceutical companies and leading hospitals. The founding institutions include Imperial College, King's College, University College, the Maudsley and Royal Marsden NHS Hospital Trusts and a leading pharmaceutical company.

The design of the cluster is based on proven models and is focused on building and reinforcing linkages and collaboration across institutions to improve innovation and competitiveness. This in turn will create a virtuous cycle attracting further resources and more opportunities for collaboration. GMEC has developed a set of agreed objectives and principles supported by processes to build collaboration, set up joint programmes, attract resources and prioritize opportunities. The aim is to provide institutions with the opportunity to identify and participate in world-class research and development opportunities, build research platforms and contribute to improved patient outcomes. There are currently (June 2007) 21 joint programmes in the launch and pre-launch phase across a range of areas.

In summary GMEC will combine with significant research capabilities of the participating institutions with strong and accelerating focus on collaboration to deliver joint world-class research and development programmes. GMEC will become one of the leading global medical clusters – but only if it keeps this drive going.

Everyone involved in healthcare in the UK – all who want to see patients better off, money better spent and a wealthier UK – needs to sign up for reform. Change is difficult for everyone, but the need for change in the UK is so obvious that it is clear that failure to reform will have serious consequences for its citizens.

Conclusion

This book has tried to analyse why the NHS, in spite of the daily dedication of clinical staff, is failing. The government has made a determined effort to solve two of the three problems that afflict the NHS: insufficient money, and no policy to drive effective resource allocation. But the government has not tackled the remaining problem – the dysfunctional NHS organization leading to the chronically poor quality of management in the NHS. This is not surprising. On the one hand, the politicians are themselves deeply inexperienced in management – they have rarely come across it in their careers. Their experience set is in creating policy, which they do quite well. It is perplexing to them that the more policy they come up with, the worse things get. They are blind to the reason why it gets worse – because they are blind to the central importance of professional management in creating effective organizational dynamics, managing efficient operations, and, in particular in the case of the NHS, managing a complex change programme. Low-quality NHS/Civil Service management is clearly not up to the task.

The organizational dynamics – central control and poor local management – produce an operating environment that detracts from the clinician-patient interface. The whole system, if it were well managed, would be designed to enhance this relationship. As it is, the dynamics detract from it – and clinicians are increasingly angry about, and dangerously disengaged from, the NHS. The purpose of this book has been to make recommendations about how we can break out of these dysfunctional dynamics. A core theme is that senior NHS and Civil Service management are not competent to bring about this change: it will require new management.

The government's policy agenda is largely good, but it needs to create a vision that gives people a psychological context to explain why they are going through the process of disorientating change. That vision is to design a healthcare economy that focuses relentlessly on improving clinical outcomes for the patients. A huge improvement is needed in the collection, analysis and publication of clinical outcome data. And then competition is to be unleashed such that the best provider – best in terms of patient interests and patient safety – gets the right to deliver the service. The government has shot itself in the foot, and invited taunts of 'privatization' by giving out small contracts to the tiny, peripheral UK private healthcare sector.

What it needs to do is to drive competition right to the core of the NHS by getting the excellent clinical units that do exist in the NHS to take over from the poorer-performing clinical units elsewhere in the country. As an ongoing process, and in order to create a real market that focuses on patient value and delivers service efficiently on behalf of the UK taxpayer, regional commissioners need to actively manage competition and improve clinical outcomes day by day.

This system will finally break down the self-interested public sector monopoly that the NHS has become. Aneurin Bevan's founding principles

– patient choice, competition among providers and clinical freedom – have been usurped by the public-sector unions. Now it is their rights, their jobs and their lack of accountability that have become paramount.

The underperforming and poorly managed NHS has not only produced poorer patient service at a higher cost than it should have done, but the Civil Service management of 'graceful decline' has also damaged the wealth of the country. And our lead in biomedical science has been seriously degraded.

The reform process has to succeed; the forces of reaction trying to subvert progress, including the complicit senior NHS/Civil Service management, have to be defeated; the system has to be driven by the patient, and the patient's rights have to be guaranteed by creating competition, so that the consequence of poor performance is a denial of the right to practice and replacement by a safer service.

The stakes are enormously high. We all have to act now.

Notes

Introduction

1. OECD (2005) *Health Data 2005*.
2. Leatherman and Sutherland, 'The Quest for Quality in the NHS', p. 79.
3. Quoted in Michael Foot, *Aneurin Bevan*, Book 2, pp. 192/3.
4. Michael Porter and Elizabeth Olmsted Teisberg, 'Redefining Competition in Health Care', *Harvard Business Review*, June 2004, p. 7.
5. Michael Foot, *Aneurin Bevan*, p. 193.

Chapter 1: The case for change

1. OECD (2005) *Health Data 2005*, October.
2. *Money in the NHS: The Facts*, NHS Confederation, September 2005.
3. Jo Revill, 'King's Fund Briefing', *Observer*, 12 December 2005.
4. It is very likely that even this figure is much less than the taxpayer will eventually pay – the commitment made by this government to public sector pensions is staggering, and the real commitment is concealed behind ridiculous actuarial assumptions that grossly underestimate the commitment.
5. King's Fund Briefing, February 2006, pp. 2, 3.
6. King's Fund Briefing, February 2006.
7. Resuscitating the NHS: A Consultant's View, Dr Maurice Slevin, Centre for Policy Studies, January 2003.
8. Resuscitating the NHS: A Consultant's View, Dr Maurice Slevin, Centre for Policy Studies, January 2003.
9. 'Financial Management in the NHS', joint report by the National Audit Office and the Audit Commission, June 2005.
10. The Hospital Guide, December 2005, published by the Dr Foster healthcare group.
11. *The Quest for Quality in the NHS*, Leatherman, S. and Sutherland, K. (2003) Nuffield Trust, London, p. 91.
12. Leatherman and Sutherland (2003), p. 78.
13. *The Quest for Quality in the NHS: A Chartbook on Quality of Care in the UK*, Leatherman, S. and Sutherland, K. and The Nuffield Trust, Radcliffe Publishing, Oxford, Seattle (2005), Chart 1.18.

14. Leatherman and Sutherland (2005), Chart 2.8.
15. Leatherman and Sutherland (2005), Chart 3.2.
16. Leatherman and Sutherland (2005), p. 115 and Chart 1.11.
17. Leatherman and Sutherland (2005), Chart 1.13.
18. Leatherman and Sutherland (2005), Chart 1.14.
19. Leatherman and Sutherland (2005), Chart 1.15.
20. Leatherman and Sutherland (2205), Chart 1.6.
21. Leatherman and Sutherland (2005), Chart 1.7.
22. Leatherman and Sutherland (2005), p. 155, and Table 9.43a.
23. Leatherman and Sutherland (2005), Chart 2.5.
24. Leatherman and Sutherland (2005), Chart 4.9.
25. Leatherman and Sutherland (2005), Chart 4.12.
26. Leatherman and Sutherland (2005), p. 85.
27. Leatherman and Sutherland (2005), pp. 91–92.
28. Leatherman and Sutherland (2005), p. 179.

Chapter 2: What is wrong with the NHS?

1. Michael Foot's biography *Aneurin Bevan*, pp. 134 and 163.
2. Alan Milburn Speech to the New Health Network, 14 January 2002.
3. Patricia Hewitt, *Guardian*, 2 July 2005.
4. Brooks Atkinson, *Once Around the Sun*, 1951.
5. 'Twenty Years On', BMJ, Leading article, 1968 – quoted from 'From Cradle to Grave', King's Fund.
6. 'The dis-alienation of the NHS', BMJ, Leading article, 1978 – quoted from 'From Cradle to Grave', King's Fund.
7. Excerpts from Ken Jarred, Sally Irvine Lecture 'The NHS – past, present and future', Tuesday 15 November 2005, IHM Annual Conference and Exhibition.
8. As note 7.
9. Anthony Brown and Gaby Hinsliff (2000), 'Patients' Champion for Every Hospital', *Observer*, 23 July – quoted from Institute of Directors (2002) 'The Mutual Health Service: How to Decentralise the NHS'.
10. John Carvel (2000), 'Virgin Team Highlights NHS Shambles', *Guardian*, 22 July.
11. Nigel Edwards (2004), 'Managers: Can the NHS manage without them?' SMF, p. 3.
12. Nigel Edwards (2004), 'Managers: Can the NHS manage without them?' SMF, p. 4.
13. Jo Revill, 'Diary of a Nurse', *Observer*, 27 November 2005.
14. Isabel Oakeshott, 'NHS money spent on management consultants', *Evening Standard*, 24 November 2005.

15. Helene Mulholland, *Guardian Unlimited*, 16 December 2005.
16. Audit Commission, p. 2, 'Early Lessons from Payment by Results', 11 October 2005.
17. OECD (2004), *Economic Survey of the United Kingdom 2004: Activity-Based Funding, Incentives and Waiting Times in Health Care*, OECD, p. 2.
18. Siciliani and Hurst 2003, quoted in OECD (2004), *Economic Survey of the United Kingdom 2004: Activity-Based Funding, Incentives and Waiting Times in Health Care*, OECD, p. 3.
19. Patricia Hewitt, 'Annual Health and Social Care Lecture', LSE, 13 December 2005.
20. OECD (2005), *Economic Survey of the United Kingdom, 2005*, OECD, p. 2.
21. Nicholas Timmins, *Financial Times*, 4 January 2006, p. 2.
22. Nicholas Timmins, *Financial Times*, 4 January 2006, p. 2.
23. Patricia Hewitt (2005), 'NHS Ahead of Schedule to Achieve Efficiency Savings', Department of Health, 6 December, p. 1.
24. Laura Donnelly (2006), *Health Service Journal*, 16 February, p. 14.
25. Alison Moore (2005), 'NHS Deficits', *Health Service Journal*, 8 December.
26. Laura Donnelly (2006), *Health Service Journal*, 16 February, p. 14.
27. Patricia Hewitt MP (2005), Annual Health and Social Care Lecture, LSE, 13 December.
28. Politics.Co.UK (2004), 'Productivity Drop off in NHS', 19 October, p. 1.
29. FT.Com (2004), 'NHS Fails Tests on Improved Efficiency', 19 October.
30. BBC News Online (2004), 'NHS is "Wasteful and Inefficient"', 19 October.
31. Public Finance (2004), 'NHS Productivity Report "misses crucial changes",' 22 October, p. 1.
32. Professor Julian Le Grand, *Guardian Unlimited* (2005), 'Market Forces are the Future of the Health Service', 26 September, p. 2.
33. National Statistics (2004), *Public Service Productivity*, October, p. 2.
34. National Audit Office and the Audit Commission (2005), 'Financial Management in the NHS', 24 June, p. 7.
35. Audit Commission (2005), 'Managing the Financial Implications of NICE Guidance', September 2005, p. 4.
36. Department of Health (2005), 'Financial Turnaround in the NHS', 25 January, p. 4.
37. Jo Revill (2006), 'NHS efficiency labelled "over-performing"', *Observer*, 5 February.
38. Ashley Seager (2006), *Guardian Unlimited*, 28 February.

39. Laura Donnelly (2006), 'NHS Deficits', *Health Service Journal*, 16 February, p. 16.
40. 'The Reluctant Managers, Part 1: Report on Reforming Whitehall', KPMG, December 2005.
41. *Avoiding Financial Flashpoints* (2000), Washington, DC: Health Care Advisory Board.
42. W. B. Schaufeli (1999) 'Burnout', in J. Firth-Cozens and R. L. Payne (eds), *Stress in Health Professionals: psychological and organizational causes and interventions*, London, Wiley.
43. Leatherman and Sutherland (2005), p. 172.

Chapter 3: A vision for the NHS

1. Michael E. Porter (1980) *Competitive Strategy: Techniques for Analyzing Industries and Competitors*, New York: The Free Press; Michael E. Porter (1985), *Competitive Advantage: Creating and Sustaining Superior Performance*, New York: The Free Press; Michael E. Porter (1985) *Beyond Competitive Advantage*, Working Paper, Harvard Graduate School of Business Administration; Michael E. Porter (ed.) (1986) *Competition in Global Industries*, Boston: Harvard Business School Press; Michael E. Porter (1987) 'From Competitive Advantage to Corporate Strategy', *Harvard Business Review*.
2. Michael E. Porter (1990) *The Competitive Advantage of Nation*, New York: The Free Press.
3. Michael E. Porter and Elizabeth Olmsted Teisberg (2006) *Redefining Healthcare: Creating Value-Based Competition on Results*, Boston: Harvard Business School Press.
4. All subsequent references in this chapter are to the same book (Porter and Teisberg).

Chapter 4: Breaking the dysfunctional dynamics

1. Quoted in Michael Foot's 'Aneurin Bevan', book 2, pp. 130/1.
2. The British Social Attitudes Survey, 22nd report (2005) National Centre for Social Research, Sage Publications.
3. Julian Le Grand, *Choice and Competition in Public Services*, Public lecture, London School of Economics, 21 February 2006.
4. Julian Le Grand, *Choice and Competition in Public Services*, Public lecture, London School of Economics, 21 February 2006.
5. Daniel Martin, *Health Services Journal*, 15 December 2005, p. 7.
6. Department of Health press release, 20 January 2006.

7. Mary-Louise Harding, HSJ, Commissioning in the NHS, 15 December 2005, p. 6.
8. Nicholas Timmins, 'NHS Reorganization', *Financial Times*, 8 March 2006, p. 2.
9. Glasgow University Survey of 1,050 practices, *British Medical Journal*, 16 December 2005.
10. Professor Paul Corrigan, 'Improving the Quality and Capacity of Primary Care', *Social Market Foundation*, November 2005, p. 6.
11. Nicholas Timmins, Reducing NHS Waiting Times, *Financial Times*, 4 December 2005, p. 2.
12. Foster Intelligence, 'Keeping People Out of Hospital: The Challenge of Reducing Emergency Admissions', February 2006, p. 4.
13. BBC News Online, 16 January 2006, p. 1
14. BBC News Online,16 January 2006.
15. Ministerial Statement by Patricia Hewitt MP, *Hansard*, 17 January 2006.
16. Professor Paul Corrigan, 'Informing Choice in Primary Care', *Social Market Foundation*, November 2005, pp. 9, 10.
17. King's Fund, *NHS Waiting Times*, 1 April 2005, p. 1.
18. Patricia Hewitt, DOH press release, 21 February 2006.
19. DoH, *Independent Sector Treatment Centres*, 16 February 2006, p. 1.
20. DoH, *Independent Sector Treatment Centres*, 16 February 2006.
21. King's Fund, *Designing the 'New' NHS: Ideas to Make a Supplier Market in Heath Care Work*. Report of an Independent Working Group, June 2006.
22. D. Osborne and T. Goebler (1992) *Reinventing Government: How the Entrepreneurial Spirit is Transforming the Public Sector*, New York: Penguin Books.

Chapter 5: Creating sustainability and building international competitiveness

1. Julian Le Grand, *Choice and Competition in Public Services*, Public lecture, London School of Economics, 21 February 2006.
2. Michael E. Porter (1990), *The Competitive Advantage of Nations*, New York: The Free Press.
3. MIT, *The Engines of Economic Growth: Study on the Social and Economic Impact of MIT*, Press release, 11 March 2003.
4. University of Maryland, *Building on Excellence: The Next Steps*, 3 May 2000, p. 2.
5. *Strategic Science Provision in English Universities*, Science and Technology Select Committee, 2005, pp. 62, 65 and 67.

6. Source as for note 5, p. 67
7. Source as for note 5, pp. 79, 85.
8. ABHI, *A Competitive Analysis of the Healthcare Industry in the UK*, June 2001, pp. 3, 4 and 5.*
9. ABHI, *A Comparative Analysis of the Healthcare Industry in the UK*, June 2001, pp. 3, 4, 5.
10. ABHI, *A Comparative Analysis of the Healthcare Industry in the UK*, June 2001, pp. 7, 8.
11. ABHI, *A Comparative Analysis of the Healthcare Industry in the UK*, June 2001, pp. 7, 8.
12. ABHI, *A Comparative Analysis of the Healthcare Industry in the UK*, June 2001, pp. 7, 8.
13. ABHI, *A Comparative Analysis of the Healthcare Industry in the UK*, June 2001, pp. 8, 9.
14. ABHI, *A Comparative Analysis of the Healthcare Industry in the UK*, June 2001, p. 9.
15. ABHI, *A Comparative Analysis of the Healthcare Industry in the UK*, June 2001, p. 10.

*   *Note*:   The ABHI analysis has been updated in a more recent publication: *Healthcare Industry Taskforce*, 17 November 2004, http://www.dh.gov.uk/en/PublicationsandStatistics/Publications/PublicationsPolicyAnd Guidance/DH_4094982.

Index